Bodde

SCRIPTURE UN

BIBLE CHARACTERS AND DOCTRINES

Adam to Esau

E. M. BLAIKLOCK, M.A., D.LITT.

The God Who Speaks—Scripture and Revelation

PHILIP CROWE, M.A.

SCRIPTURE UNION
5 WIGMORE STREET
LONDON, W1H0AD

First published 1971

I SBN 0 242 85421 6

Printed and bound in Ireland by
Cahill & Co. Limited, Dublin

Scripture Union Bible Characters and Doctrines

INTRODUCTION

This series of S.U. Bible study aids takes its place alongside our existing range of Notes and Bible Study Books.

Each volume of Bible Characters and Doctrines is divided into the right number of sections to make daily use possible, though dates are not attached to the sections because of the books' continuing use as a complete set of character studies and doctrinal expositions. The study for each day is clearly numbered and the Bible passage to be read is placed alongside it.

Sections presenting the characters and doctrines alternate throughout each book, providing balance and variety in the selected subjects. At the end of each section there is a selection of questions and themes for further study related to the material covered in the preceding readings.

Each volume will provide material for one quarter's use, with between 91 and 96 sections. Where it is suggested that two sections should be read together in order to fit the three-month period, they are marked with an asterisk.

The scheme will be completed in four years. Professor E. M. Blaiklock, who writes all the character studies, will work progressively through the Old and New Testament records. Writers of the doctrinal sections contribute to a pattern of studies drawn up by the Rev. Geoffrey Grogan, Principal of the Bible Training Institute, Glasgow, in his capacity as Co-ordinating Editor. A chart overleaf indicates how the doctrinal sections are planned.

In this series biblical quotations are normally taken from the RSV unless otherwise identified. Occasionally Professor Blaiklock provides his own translation of the biblical text.

DOCTRINAL STUDY SCHEME

	Year 1	Year 2	Year 3	Year 4
First Quarter	The God who Speaks	Man and Sin	The Work of Christ	The Kingdom and the Church
Second Quarter	God in His World	Law and Grace	Righteousness in Christ	The Mission of the Church
Third Quarter	The Character of God	The Life of Christ	Life in Christ	The Church's Ministry and Ordinances
Fourth Quarter	The Holy Trinity	The Person of Christ	The Holy Spirit	The Last Things

DOCTRINAL STUDIES

THE GOD WHO SPEAKS

Study

The God who Speaks

1	'In many ways'	Hebrews 1.1–2.1
2	In Creation	Isaiah 45
3	In Conscience	Romans 2.1–16
4	In History	Genesis 15
5	In Law	Psalm 19

The God who Speaks—in Prophets

14	The Mediums and the Message	Deuteronomy 18.9–22
15	Balaam	Numbers 24
16	Micaiah	I Kings 22.1–28
17	Prophecy Lost	Amos 7.10–8.12
18	Prophecy Regained	Joel 2.21–29

The God who Speaks—in Christ

27	The Word of God	John 1.1–18
28	God's Word and Christ's Ministry	Luke 4.16–37
29	God's Word and Christ's Teaching	John 8.21–30
30	Christ—the Heart of God's Word	Acts 2.22–39
31	'Seen and heard'	1 John 1.1–2.6
32	'This is the message'	1 John 1.5–2.6

The Jews, the Scriptures and the Messiah

41	Delight in the Law	Psalm 119.129–144
42	Inspired and Profitable	2 Timothy 3.10–17
43	Prophetic Inspiration	2 Peter 1.12–2.3
44	Tradition versus Life	Mark 7.1–13

CHARACTER STUDIES
ADAM TO ESAU

Study		
6	Adam the First Man	Genesis 1.26–31
7	Adam's Responsibility	Genesis 2.7–15
8	Adam's Rebellion	Genesis 2.16–20
9	Eve the First Woman	Genesis 2.21–3.6
10	Adam and Eve	Genesis 3.7–4.2
11	Cain the First Killer	Genesis 4.3–15
12	Lamech the Second Killer	Genesis 4.17–25
13	Enoch, who Walked with God	Genesis 5.18–24
19	Noah, who Obeyed God	Genesis 6.9–8.19
20	Noah's Lapse	Genesis 9
21	Abraham of Ur	Hebrews 11.8–22
22	Abraham and God	Genesis 12.1–3; Acts 7.1–8
23	Abraham's Father	Joshua 24.1–5
24	Abraham's Retreat	Genesis 12.10–20
25	Abraham's Return	Genesis 13.1–7; Romans 4.1–8
26	Abraham's Faith	Genesis 13.8–18
33	Lot	Luke 17.22–32
34	Abraham's Raid	Genesis 14.1–16; 2 Corinthians 6.11–18
35	Abraham's Friend	Genesis 14.17–20; Hebrews 7.1–10
36	Abraham and the King of Sodom	Genesis 14.21–24
37	Reaction	Genesis 15
38	Abraham and Hagar	Genesis 16
39	Abraham and the Covenant	Genesis 17
40	Abraham the Host	Genesis 18

THE GOD WHO SPEAKS

Introduction

'The Alexandria Quartet' is a large, single work of literature which is made up of four separate, interlocking books. In his Preface, Lawrence Durrell explains that 'if the axis of the work has been properly laid down, it should be possible to radiate from it in any direction'. A roughly similar pattern is necessary in studying Christian faith. To be complete and relevant to life, it must have four parts, properly related to one another.

One is the close and careful study of the separate parts of Scripture. Another is relating those parts to one another, to build up a complete understanding. A third is to study the life and faith of other Christians and the life of the world. The fourth is to apply Christian truth, first to oneself, and then to others and to society. All four are essential to those who would be disciples of Christ—that is, Christ's pupils.

Clearly all four lines of the axis cannot be followed at the same time, though one is always likely to illuminate the others. In studies such as this book provides, it is necessary to concentrate primarily on the close study of separate passages of the Bible. Many things that could be said about God, revelation, and the Bible in a different kind of book, a book of systematic theology for instance, are necessarily omitted. No more than hints at the other three lines of study can be offered, hints which will, it is hoped, start movements of thought in all sorts of directions.

The nine groups of Bible doctrine studies in this book fall into three main sections. The first three are concerned with 'The God who Speaks', in creation and law, in the prophets, and in Christ. The next three examine the attitude to the O.T. Scriptures of the Jews, of Christ, and of the Apostles. The last three are concerned with our attitude to the Bible, its authority, its interpretation, and our obedience to the God who speaks through it.

The God who Speaks

1 : 'In many ways'

Hebrews 1.1–2.1

At 6.54 B.S.T. on the evening of 17th April, 1970, millions of people around the world paused, anxious, listening intently. After a few minutes' silence, the voice of Jack Swigert was heard. 'O.K. Joe!' Just two words, and the world knew that the crew of Apollo 13 were alive and still in control after a flight which was so nearly a disaster.

'Why is God silent?' people ask. 'Just a few words, and we would know that He is alive and in control.' It is no new question.

> *'And all night long we have not stirred,*
> *And yet God has not said a word!'*

says one of Browning's characters.

The answer to the question is in Heb. **1**. 'God has spoken.' He has made Himself known by the things He has said. Man has not discovered God, nor has he come to the conclusion, on the basis of logical deduction, that God exists. The initiative has been taken by God. He has spoken.

The phrase 'in many and various ways' may be translated 'in many degrees and in different ways', but the writer to the Hebrews does not mention the way in which God has shown Himself in creation and in history. He concentrates on the words of God because without His word to guide our understanding, neither creation nor history would have divine meaning for man.

The word spoken 'in these last days' (2) stands in contrast

to the word spoken 'of old'; it fulfils and supersedes it. The revelation of God in Christ is complete (the tense of 'He has spoken' indicates an action complete in the past), while the revelation through the prophets was fragmentary. And what God has done in Christ is for all time, whereas the prophets spoke 'of old'. The phrase 'in these last days' does not mean 'recently', but 'for this period between the birth of Christ and the end of this world' (cf. Acts **17**.30 f., 2 Pet. **3**.1–4). Christ is the Word of God for *our* age. The risen, living Christ is God's Word now. In Christ, God has said all there is to say. The question 'Why is God silent?' is meaningless. The question is—'Will man listen to what God has said and still says to our age through Jesus Christ?' And for those who have heard, there is a clear and unusually strong exhortation to give what might be paraphrased as 'an absolute excess of attention' to it (**2**.1).

2 : In Creation

Isaiah 45

The works of God in creation are plain for all men to see. Anyone and everyone can see the growth of plants and the life of animals, the sun, the moon and the seas. Yet to the vast majority of people, the wealth of creation does not inspire a song of praise like Psa. **103** or **104**—'O Lord, how manifold are thy works! In wisdom hast thou made them all.' Instead, people believe the sun to be a god or are terrified by unseen powers in the world which they attempt to placate, or they abuse the earth's resources in a grasping materialism.

The truth is that God still speaks to men through the creation, but because of sin, men cannot hear. Isa. **45**.18 f. links some of the plainest statements in Scripture about the God who speaks to the great facts of creation. Three assertions about creation (18) are paralleled by three statements about God and His word (18b, 19). The climax is in v. 19b—'I the Lord speak the truth, I declare what is right.' All this is in stark contrast to the silence of dumb idols, who even have to be carried to safety when heathen nations are defeated (20).

There is a similar forthrightness in Paul's statements about creation in Rom. **1**.18–23. What can be known about God is plain, he argues; 'his invisible nature, namely, his eternal power and deity, has been clearly perceived in the things that have been made' (20).

God's power and deity are also evident in the earlier verses of Isa. **45** which speak of creation (5–12). For man, the creature, to strive with the Almighty Creator is absurd (9). His power is absolute, beyond challenge (11 f.). But that power is also personal. The personal analogies of v. 10 would be grossly inappropriate to the heathen deities and the man-made idols, and the reference to 'my children' in v. 11 implies a personal relationship.

There is an echo, at least, of the word of God in creation, in the experience of a seven-year-old Muslim boy travelling home with his father after his first year at a Christian school. 'There is nothing more beautiful in Yezd,' he wrote later, when he became Bishop in Iran, 'than its sky at night, and its gorgeous mountains in the early morning and in the evening, with the effect of light and shade on them. I remember that, while sitting on the donkey continuing our journey, I started to recite verses about the 8th Psalm: "O Lord, our Lord, how majestic is thy name in all the earth!"'

3 : In Conscience

Romans 2.1–16

In 'The Child's World', Phyllis Hostler discusses modern attempts to 'discard or at least to soften' the idea of conscience. 'But it happens,' she writes, 'that like many other of our grandparents' ideas which we have once discarded, the idea of conscience has returned vigorous as ever. Most of us who have had dealings with little children would assert that if naughtiness is natural, so also are guilt-feelings—that is to say, both arise within the individual without our help.'

Paul's argument in Rom. **2**.1–16 is based on two assertions about man's awareness of right and wrong. The first is that everyone has a conscience (15). The same assertion is clearly implied in Rom. **13**.5, and in many of the other 32 N.T. passages in which conscience is mentioned (cf. 1 Cor. **8**, 1 Tim. **4**.2). All men have been created by God with an inbuilt moral radar system, whether they describe it in the vivid words of an African as 'a sharp knife in the belly', or in the terms of medieval theologians as 'the voice of God in the soul'.

The second assertion is explained in relation to the law of God (12 f.). What God said in the law, which 'was added because of transgressions' (Gal. 3.19), He had said previously in creating man with a moral awareness (14, 15a). Paul is as acutely conscious of the effect of the Fall as anyone. His statements about the grim, universal reality of sin are as strong as any written. Yet he can still argue that Gentiles, who have no knowledge of what God has said in the law, can show that 'what the law requires is written on their hearts' (15).

It is thus clear from this passage that in giving all men a moral awareness and a conscience, God has spoken. The Jews may have the law, the oracles of God (3.2), but in the last analysis, Jews and Gentiles are equal before God. He 'shows no partiality' (11). He has spoken to all men.

It must be recognized that it is the gift of conscience itself which may be described, not altogether satisfactorily, as 'the voice of God in the soul'. People may respond to or 'train' their conscience in different ways, but that does not alter the fact that God has given man the capacity to be aware of right and wrong. Conscience is like an alarm-clock—people may switch it off and go back to sleep, but the clock is still there.

For meditation : 'The absolute pitch of the trained musician is akin to the absolute moral pitch of the trained Christian : the wrong note, be it never so little wrong, causes immediate pain' (C. A. Pierce, Conscience in the N.T.).

4 : In History

Genesis 15

For all we know, there may have been many families in the city of Ur of the Chaldeans who decided to pack up all their belongings and move out. Their departure was real and important, both to them and to God. Yet it is Abraham's move which is decisively important for world history, and the reason for this is crucial to our understanding of revelation. Abraham's move was based on the command, the promises and the explanations which God gave. All three are in Gen. **15**.

The command is referred to in v. 7 (cf. **12**.1). The promise, first given in **12**.2, which Abraham had begun to doubt as he had got older (8), is renewed in vs. 5 f. and 17–21. The explanation is only hinted at in vs. 12–16 and in the promises; it was not given in full until much later (cf. Rom. **4**). It was the command and the promise of God that mattered more to Abraham (cf. Gen. **22**.1–3, 12, 15–19; Isa. **45**.9).

God speaks in the events of history, which He directs and controls, in the promises which frequently accompany those events, and in the interpretation of the events which He gives. Events on their own may or may not speak to man of God's providence in general terms. It is event and interpretation together which constitute God's revelation of Himself through history.

Gen. **15** does not in fact describe any event at all; the whole chapter is God telling Abraham about past and future events. In view of some modern theories about revelation, it is important to note that Gen. **15** records what God told Abraham about events, and not what Abraham thought about them (1, 7, 13, 18). A widely-held view of revelation is that 'There is no such thing as revealed truth', only 'propositions which express the results of correct thinking concerning revelation' (William Temple). In other words, Scripture contains inspired attempts to understand the divine meaning in events: the phrase 'the word of the Lord came to Abraham' really means, 'Abraham's understanding of what God would have said if He had spoken at all is . . .' Interpreting Scripture then becomes a matter of reconstructing the event and assessing the extent to which the given interpretation of it is true.

Against this view, Scripture claims to be the revealed truth of God. It records what God has done and what He has said about it. The Biblical view is of a personal God, a God who speaks to men.

5 : In Law

Psalm 19

'One of the greatest lyrics in the world', is how C. S. Lewis describes this psalm. Its six verses about nature, five about law and four about man are an anthem of praise to the God who speaks in these three ways. For the psalmist, the connection between the sections is so close and natural that he passes from one to the other without pause or hesitation.

Perowne suggests that the psalmist may perhaps have been gazing at the first flush of an Eastern sunrise. He looks up at the glory of the sky. He watches the sun, and then begins to feel the heat, which develops into 'blinding, tyrannous rays hammering the hills, searching every cranny'. Nothing escapes it (6). 'Then at once, in verse 7, he is talking of something else, which hardly seems to him something else because it is so like the all-piercing, all-detecting sunshine. The law is undefiled, the law gives light, it is clean and everlasting, it is "sweet". No one can improve on this and nothing can more fully admit us to the old Jewish feeling about the law; luminous, severe, disinfectant, exultant' (Lewis).

Each line of vs. 7–9 contains a different noun to denote God's word in the law and a different adjective to describe it, followed by a separate phrase to indicate its effect. The three verses are a marvel of economy in words and rich variety in meaning—the envy of any modern poet! Nor does the symmetry end there. Six times in these verses the psalmist mentions the divine name, and at the final climax of the psalm he brings it up to what was considered to be the perfect number, seven, unobtrusively emphasizing the perfection of divine revelation.

For generations, many Christians have sung this psalm on Christmas Day. Praise to God for His word in creation and in the law prepares them to worship the Word made flesh.

For meditation: Close study of God's words leads the psalmist to pay attention to his own (14).

Questions and themes for study and discussion on Studies 1–5

1. How complete is the knowledge of God which creation and conscience reveal, and how much can man appreciate of that revelation?
2. Is 'the voice of God in the soul' a good description of conscience? (There are not too many N.T. references to look up!)

CHARACTER STUDIES

6 : Adam the First Man

Genesis 1.26–31

No one knows how many thousands of years ago it was, but at some point in time Man appeared in an earthly Paradise. He was Adam, and he moves into the first pages of the Bible, a true human being, recognizably one of us, innocent, at peace with God, and happy. God, says the Bible, with sublime simplicity, 'created man in His own image'. Man still, even in his fallen state, finds within himself the same sort of reason which expresses itself in the universe. Without that assumption all scientific investigation would be impossible. The first mark of Adam in the plain, brief pages which open the Bible is intelligence. At his first appearance he is without all arts and crafts, but is challenged to an intelligent obedience to God (Gen. **2**.15–17); he is entrusted with responsibility, on the assumption that he is able intelligently to bear it (Gen. **1**.28–30); he has the gift of language, in which man gives expression not only to his reason, but also to his imagination (Gen. **2**.19). Here quite obviously is man endowed with all that which makes man unique. Man's distinctive being consists in knowing himself to be God's creation, known of God and knowing Him. In his very creation is a summons to listen, to understand, and to believe. Unlike all else in the created universe, man is a citizen of two worlds. Though part of God's creation, and participating in it, man stands, like God, over against the physical world and is, in consequence, its divinely appointed master. He is in the world but something other than the world. That is why he can create within the physical world that which is other than the world-culture, the work of his mind and spirit. That is why man can rule. Man's distinctiveness is not in the power of his body, or the acuteness of his senses, in both of which he falls notably short of other creatures, but in the fact that he stands 'in God's image', having understanding of God's thought, purpose and will. This is precisely how Adam is described. Nothing so far has marred the beauty of his life. His happiness flows from unclouded fellowship. God takes joy in him, and he in God. It is a picture soon to fade.

7 : Adam's Responsibility

Genesis 2.7–15

Every man is a volume, someone has remarked, if we know how to read it. This is eminently true of Adam. All man's potentialities, all his vast opportunity, and all his capacity for failure, are to be read in him. He is given dominion over all the created world, and all subordinate creatures. Concerning the Garden, he is told 'to till it and keep it'. The two words go together, and measure man's responsibility. Adam no doubt understood it quite literally. He was to give back to the earth what he took from it. Man, and it is part of the Fall which is now looming large in the tragic Genesis story, has learned that part of his task which feeds his pride. He has tilled the earth, bent Nature to his ends, and tamed her. Perhaps in the process he has already destroyed her. Read the first half of Isa. **24**. The earth, says the prophet, is defiled under its own inhabitants, because they have broken eternal laws. One such law is that man gives in proportion as he receives, that duty and privilege go together. God put Adam in his earthy Eden, 'to *serve* and *keep* it' (Gen. **2**.15). Adam was master, but, like any true master, he ruled only in proportion as he served; he had to keep the garden, i.e. 'care for it' (NEB). How many long years Adam lived in happiness, seeking to serve God and God's creation, and discovering in the process that the created world, on such terms, served him, we do not know. The brief account, in the language of far centuries, tells us no more than we need to know. We are, none the less, left with the impression of Adam's unique Godlikeness, his easy bearing of the load of a lordship unknown on the earth before. 'The most important thought I ever had,' wrote Daniel Webster, 'was that of my individual responsibility to God.' Adam bore the load joyously and well while obedience was in the forefront of his life. 'No man doth safely rule,' said Thomas à Kempis, 'but he that hath learned gladly to obey.' Such was Adam, God's regent on earth, in the years of his innocence. The time of that innocence extended into the years of fellowship with Eve. Chapter **2** closes with God's image still visible in Adam.

8 : Adam's Rebellion

Genesis 2.16–20

Part of God's image in man is moral. This does not mean that fallen man is morally like God. It simply maintains that to be aware of the ethical imperative is part of man's constitution. Reason leads man not only to principles of knowledge but also to laws of conduct. He also possesses the power of self-decision. It is this which most clearly constituted Adam a Person. Alone in Creation man is faced constantly with the call to moral decision. It is a condition born of his responsibility. No one can deprive him of his power of deciding for himself. The only Power which could force him to say 'yes' will not do so, because the act of compulsion would alter the constitution of man, and deny the fundamental principle of his creation. God left Adam free to make his choice. Man's present constitution, for all the arguments of modern sophistry, is clear. Man is free. The power to decide has been conferred upon him, and that power is continually stirred and renewed by God's call. Inescapable, more than the air we breathe, is the law that man must decide, as long as he lives, and at every moment of his life. If man could escape that necessity he would cease to be man.

Adam was the second human being to be faced with temptation. Eve was the first, and to that subject we shall return in the next study. He was called to decide, wavered before the right decision, and made the wrong one. The act loosed sin upon the human race. It visibly loosed sin in Adam. He allowed his love for Eve to lead him astray (Gen. 3.6), and yet was small enough to blame Eve for the seduction (12), and even to turn, with argument perilously close to modern theories which diminish or deny free-will, to blaming God. It was 'the woman God gave him' which initiated harm. It was, in other words, a situation for which God was responsible! With broken fellowship came loss of innocence, and shame (10). What opportunity Adam, at this point of failure, lost, for, as Penn said, 'to be innocent is to be not guilty, but to be virtuous is to overcome our evil inclinations'. It could have been, as all victory is, a great leap forward for his humanity.

9 : Eve the First Woman

Genesis 2.21–3.6

If Adam is recognizably man, Eve is as recognizably woman. The fellowship of the first couple is complete. Their sin and their shame are mutual, and there is pathos in this. In the untold pages of the story, some of them magnificently imagined by Milton in *Paradise Lost,* joy, worship and fellowship with God must have been equally shared. Part of the deep sadness of their story is the real worth of Adam's and Eve's love, each for the other.

It is easy to trace the steps which led to sin. Curiosity was roused by the temptation. Eve stopped and looked. She reflected and talked, when she should have fled. John, in some of the last pages of the Bible to be written, speaks of temptation, and they throw vivid light on aspects of human character. Eve was human and had the wherewithal to sin. 'Everything in the world,' wrote John, 'the lust of the flesh, the lust of the eyes, and the proud glory of life, is not of the Father, but of the world' (1 John **2**.16). The 'lust which the flesh feels', to paraphrase the word, is the desire for unlawful indulgence. The eyes, undisciplined, treacherous, minister to this inward urge. Then comes 'the pride of life', 'the braggart boast of life', or however the difficult phrase may be rendered, the ostentation of the human heart, its desire for eminence not earned by goodness, its self-exaltation.

To all these sides of man's or woman's nature the Tempter made appeal. Eve need not have fallen. She was under no compulsion, for, as commentators have pointed out, the threefold classification includes all sources of sin, and finds parallel illustration in the temptations of Eve and the Lord. First, 'the lust of the flesh'. Compare, 'the tree was good for food', and 'command that these stones become bread'. Compare secondly, 'it was a delight to the eyes', with the spectacular display of 'cast yourself down'. Lastly, 'the tree was to be desired to make one wise'. Satan offered 'all the kingdoms of the world and the glory of them' . . .

A fateful and fatal moment. When woman stands firm, evil cringes. Wrote Milton:

Abash'd the Devil stood,
And felt how awful goodness is, and saw
Virtue in her shape how lovely . . .

When woman fell:

Earth felt the wound, and Nature from her seat
Sighing through all her works gave sign of woe
That all was lost . . .

10 : Adam and Eve

Genesis 3.7–4.2

The last chapter of the story of Adam and Eve is a sad one, yet, if we look with live imagination at the few brief words which tell it, a story shot through with beauty. Much survived moral disaster, for atonement had been made. Their mutual love is still evident, and Milton, in his magnificent story of the event, stresses this fact. To face all life can bring of exile, pain and toil, with someone faithful at one's side, is one of God's vast benedictions. This blessing Adam and Eve knew:

The world was all before them, where to choose
Their place of rest, and Providence their guide :
They hand in hand with wandering steps and slow
Through Eden took their solitary way.

Eden was lost, but not God. God's guidance, the fruit of His combined wisdom and love, as Milton's insight saw, was still theirs. They were now more recognizably like us, their fallen posterity, than ever. They knew good and evil, and the price of that knowledge is the understanding of sorrow and harsh toil. Nature now, once the ally, was hostile (Gen. 3.17 f.). It demanded labour to surrender that which, in the Golden Age, it had given spontaneously.

Knowing evil, they also knew the tension of strife with evil. There was 'enmity between the seed of the serpent and the seed of the woman', that ancient battle which we all know every day. In the brief story there is no evidence that Adam, and also Eve, did not win in the conflict which sprang from their first disobedience. They had known God in close and wondrous intimacy, and the memory, if not some continuance of its reality, must have coloured life, and given them, even in their exile, a graciousness beyond the ordinary.

Like the vase in which roses
Have once been distilled,
You may break, you may shatter
The vase if you will,
But the scent of the roses
Will cling to it still.

And knowing evil, they were to know too, in eternal fellowship with all who have known the anguish of evil in their own household, the fact that sin is not confined to one generation. They saw the Fall, and lived long enough to see the Fall continue its blight upon mankind. They gave life to Abel, but also to Cain.

11 : Cain the First Killer

Genesis 4.3–15

The first death in the world was murder. Abel, the victim of Cain's violence, is a shadowy figure. He was the first shepherd, that ancient stock of the nomad hinterlands which was to produce some of the best men of the Bible, and whose age-old calling was to provide imagery in Scripture from the days of Moses' desert training to Psa. **23**, and the Lord Himself (John **10**). Like some humble shepherd of the wilderness, Abel slips into the story, makes his offering, and meets his fate.

Cain stands full length. Jealousy is the first mark of him. It is commonly stated that Abel's offering found acceptance because it contained the symbolism of death for sin, which was to be so prominent a feature of the Law, and this may indeed be true. But such offerings as Cain brought are not without a place in the system yet to be, and is not the likelier reason for Cain's rejection Cain himself? 'The acceptance of the offering,' wrote Marcus Dods, 'depends on the acceptance of the offerer . . . God looks through the offering to the state of the soul from which it proceeds.'

Cain was probably already hostile to his brother. The quarrel between them merely found a focus in religion. Jealousy always grows from fear of another's superiority, and Cain saw his brother, a gentler soul, as a challenge to some form of untamed and unsurrendered violence in himself. There is some evidence that the murder was premeditated. In translating v. 8 the NEB makes Cain say: 'Let us go into the open country.' There Abel would have little fear. It was his own native sheepland. And there, unsuspecting, he was attacked and killed. Jealousy begat anger, and anger is a form of madness. And anger, as the Lord pointed out, is the seedbed of violence and murder Matt. 5.21 f.).

Cain was the first hard and unrepentant man. He went out from God's presence with something less than the punishment which he first feared (4.14 f.), but with dull resentment about the consequences of the deed which he had done. Such is the unreasoning response of rebels. No deed is complete in itself. No evil act can be confined to the hour of its doing. Sin is eminently productive. Each act of wickedness forms a link in a chain, which, unless God breaks it in grace, tangles with eternity.

12 : Lamech the Second Killer

Genesis 4.17–25

Sin, we have remarked, cannot be confined to its place and time. The brief record of Cain's line shows how it endures 'to the third and fourth generation'. The line of Cain was a line of able men. Lamech had the advantage of an emerging technology. There is only one recorded utterance of this arrogant man, one deed in the record. The deed is murder, the utterance is one of godless pride.

Verses 23 and 24 show how the tradition of Cain was maintained. Out of Cain's story was extracted one detail, the protection which was, in God's grace accorded to him, in spite of his dire sin. And now, presuming on that, as though it was some special privilege earned and granted, Lamech professes a greater immunity, doubtless through the working of metals which was becoming the monopoly of his tribe (22).

In his words, Lamech's character emerges in its completeness—violent, self-reliant, godless. He has slain a man for wounding him. He puts the boast in poetry, for the Hebrew is rhythmic and contains that parallelism of ideas which is the feature of such poetry.

I have slain a man for wounding me,
A young man for striking me,
If Cain is avenged sevenfold,
Truly Lamech seventy-sevenfold.

This is chanted to his wives, perhaps to the musical accompaniment of Jubal's lyre and pipes (21).

Let the world, and his wives, the threat implies, beware. It is to be blow for blow, eleven times more effective than God's guarantee of Cain. Cain at least felt some need of God. Lamech feels none. His swift right hand, and his tribe's power will protect him,

. . . all valiant dust that builds on dust
And guarding calls not Thee to guard . . .

'The pride of life', which Eve sensed in the first temptation, and which prompted the ancestor to murder, prompts the descendant to the second murder, compounded with blasphemous self-sufficiency. The story horrified the parallel line of Seth, and the insolent Lamech's words were preserved in the oral record, which perhaps with Abraham became the written one.

So Lamech passes from the page of history. If 'they that take the sword perish by the sword', we can be sure that he reaped the harvest of his defiance, arrogance and violent pride. The story does not consider his end worth recording. It turns to Seth, whose descendant Enoch, contemporaneous with Lamech of Cain's line, 'walked with God'.

13 : Enoch, who Walked with God

Genesis 5.18–24

With Enoch, whose whole biography is compassed likewise in four verses, we find Paradise Regained. Lamech's character stood out, lurid and unrelieved by any tint of goodness, in his taunt-song. Enoch is known to us in four words: 'Enoch walked with God.' That brief sentence merits a good man a place in any study of the characters of the Bible. It is not often that a man passes from this earth and leaves behind him nothing but a testimony of good. In most men there is the damaging exception—

They have much wisdom, yet they are not wise,
They have much goodness, yet they do not well.
Much valour, yet life mocks it with some spell.

'Naaman, commander of the army of the king of Syria, was a great man with his master and in high favour . . . *but* he was a leper.' Some such adversative clause caps all eulogy of man. Nor is the glum ending confined to the statements of theology. It is apparent in history. The Greeks invented democracy, *but* their history illustrates and documents democracy's decay and fall. Rome was given to rule the world, *but* was unable to save her empire. The Jews gave us the Old Testament, *but* crucified Christ. The twentieth century was heralded with guns and bells as the coming golden age of progress and plenty *but* . . .

Doubtless Enoch bore the scars of the Fall. The record does not claim that Enoch was sinless. All, however, that men remembered of him was the unruffled tranquillity of one whose whole life was lived in awareness that he was not alone, that One walked beside him 'every step, every mile of the way'. When the life is committed to God, and God's Spirit indwells the core of one's being, then, and only then, is one led 'in the paths of righteousness for his name's sake'.

Enoch had learned the secret. Perhaps a store of spiritual truth, a heritage of deep wisdom from Adam and Eve who had also walked with God, found fruitful harbourage in the life of Adam's descendant. Suddenly Enoch was gone, and men remembered how he had never done other than seek God's will, and had been before them the very image and pattern of his Friend. They could draw only one conclusion. The intimacy begun was consummated. The path trodden so consistently and well had turned upwards and disappeared.

Questions and themes for study and discussion on Studies 6–13

1. What recognizable traces of 'the image of God' are visible in man?
2. What do you find in the story of Eden to support 'conservation'?
3. Why and how is 'responsibility' an essential facet of character?
4. In what way was Adam a 'reasonable being'?
5. What did (a) the Lord, (b) Paul, teach about temptation?
6. What do Adam and Eve teach us about marriage?
7. What is the basis of jealousy?
8. What is the attitude of the Bible to violence?
9. How do we walk with God? Scan the Epistle to the Ephesians.

THE GOD WHO SPEAKS

The God who Speaks—in Prophets

14 : The Mediums and the Message

Deuteronomy 18.9–22

One of the remarkable features of the Bible is the way in which passages which seem obscure or irrelevant to one generation take on fresh meaning to another. When Matthew Henry wrote Volume I of his famous commentary on the Bible in 1701, he said little about vs. 9–14 of this passage, except to express amazement that even slight remains of such practices could be found in a Christian country. Today, a serial magazine on Myth and Magic is an outstanding commercial success. Ouija boards are sold as toys and used by schoolchildren; and in one week, after a court case in which four teenagers were convicted of desecrating a churchyard for a Black Mass, no less than 28 young people went to a Christian minister for help because they also had been dabbling in witchcraft.

The practices of the pagan nations in Palestine were incomparably worse than this, involving such terrible evils as child sacrifice (10), but though different in degree, they were similar in essence to the black magic and witchcraft practised today. The Bible does not put a hollow 'no' against such practices, leaving a dangerous vacuum (cf. Matt. **12**.43–45). The verses which are so clearly and strongly against 'these abominable practices' (12) should never be studied or taught on their own. The whole passage, vs. 9–22, is one unit; v. 15 follows immediately on v. 14. The Lord does not allow soothsayers or diviners because He has something far better for the people—His own word spoken clearly by a prophet. The extent to which the initiative in prophecy is taken by God is strongly emphasized. He raises up the prophet (15, 18); He gives the prophet the words to speak (18); and He is responsible for what happens to those who ignore the words of the prophet (19).

Verse 16 can only be understood in relation to Exod. **20**. 18 f. and that passage expresses the thoughts of a people deeply conscious of God's holiness and of their own sin. They wanted a prophet as a go-between. Moses himself, while serving in that capacity, looked forward to a better time when all the Lord's people would be prophets (cf. Num. **11**.26–30), a time which, in the goodness of God, we now enjoy.

15 : Balaam

Numbers 24

The story of Balaam is one of the most vivid and perplexing illustrations of prophecy that the O.T. contains. He lumbers into the history of Israel astride his renowned talking ass, a heathen diviner one minute and a prophet of God the next. He blesses when he is paid to curse, resolutely holding to God's word. Then he does a complete volte-face, and gives advice which leads to Israel's downfall and his own death, and to him being pilloried in the N.T. as a character of shame.

The parallels between Deut. **18**.15–22 and Balaam are significant. Balaam was not one of the children of Israel but a diviner belonging to one of the heathen nations (cf. Deut. **18**.14 and Num. **22**.7); yet he believed in the Lord God (Num. **22**.8) though perhaps also in other gods. In spite of this, God 'raised him up' (Deut. **18**.15) to be a prophet on Israel's behalf. Throughout the whole incident, while Balaam swung like a pendulum between God and Balak, God had final control of him. When Balaam eventually spoke, he spoke the words of blessing which God put into his mouth (**22**.35; **23**.12, 16, 26; **24**.2 f. 12 f., cf. Deut. **18**.18). Even though Balak paraded him from one place to another, hoping that the change of site would change Balaam's message or set him studying heathen omens again (**23**.13–15; **24**.1), Balaam remained steadfast. But the parallel with Deut. **18** does not end with the fact that God chose him and spoke His word through him. Balaam also spoke words God had not commanded him to speak, or perhaps he had reverted to heathen divination (Deut. **18**.20). He suggested that Israel might be seduced into heathen worship at Peor (Num. **31**.16, Rev. **2**.14) and in the war this advice eventually caused, he died (Num. **31**.8, cf. Deut. **18**.20).

Apart from providing an illustration of Deut. **18**, Balaam is an example of a man being used by God without being dedicated to Him. God could and did choose a heathen diviner to be a prophet. He spoke through him. Yet God did not force Balaam into permanent submission, and he remained an erratic, unstable character. We can only conclude that it was by his own choice that he was the sort of character the N.T. holds up to us as a warning.

For meditation: 'I do not want to preach to others, and then to find that I myself have failed to stand the test' (1 Cor. 9.27, Barclay).

16 : Micaiah

1 Kings 22.1–28

Being a true prophet was a hazardous, unpredictable calling which might involve death, prison, or glory. Being a false prophet was a different matter altogether. When Jehoshaphat wanted advice, it was a matter of moments to assemble no less than 400 'court' prophets. They were like a diplomatic corps, or like courtiers waiting on a monarch. Their chief concern was to provide impressive arguments to support what their paymasters had apparently decided to do; then as now, people did not want the truth so much as encouragement to pursue the goals they had already set for themselves.

In stark contrast, Micaiah is a vivid illustration of the true prophet of Deut. **18**, and a more 'conventional' one than Balaam. He too was raised up by God. He had the courage to stand against the king, the authorities, and all the massed ranks of false prophets. He had true prophetic conviction, expressed in the classic declaration of vs. 14 and 17–23. And he was content to rest the truth or error of his prophecy on the test set out in Deut. **18**.21 f. (28). What became of him when his prophecy was fulfilled, we do not know.

The contrast between Micaiah and the false prophets recurs repeatedly in the O.T. The true prophets denounced the false ones with great vigour, both for their errors and their greed (cf. Mic. **3**.5, 11; Jer. **14**.14 f.). It is Jeremiah who uses one most striking word to expose the heart of the difference. In Jer. **23**.18, 21 f., he denounces the prophets who scurry around with no message, and says that 'if they had stood in my *council*, then they would have proclaimed my words'. The same Hebrew word for council is used in Psa. **25**.14 ('friendship'); Psa. **55**.14 ('sweet converse'), and Amos **3**.7 ('secret'). It denotes the close, intimate fellowship of God's heavenly council. Then as now, those who declare the true word of God are those who sit in His council, listening to Him.

17 : Prophecy Lost

Amos 7.10–8.12

It is a remarkable fact, just slightly ironical perhaps, that a sermon of an obscure shepherd, which spoke of a famine of hearing the word of God (8.11), should have been preserved for over two and a half thousand years. Amos prophesied sometime in the reign of Jeroboam II (786–746 BC). It was at a time of considerable material prosperity. Amos sees the people as 'idle sprawlers, luxuriating in their choice lamb and veal, improvising their decadent music, pickling themselves in alcohol, and regaling themselves with the finest cosmetics' (Heaton; cf. **6**.1, 4–7). As sometimes happens in times of prosperity, the formal religious life of Israel was flourishing. Not surprisingly, then, there was a sharp clash between the formal, institutional, temple religion and the unconventional, earthy, disturbing, inspired ministry of Amos.

Underlying this exchange between Amaziah, priest of the temple, and Amos, prophet of God, lay the conflict between true and false prophets (10–17). Amaziah imagines that Amos is just another professional prophet who would benefit from learning wisdom and good manners in the provinces before trying to set up in practice in the capital. Amos' reply is revealing. He says that he does not belong to any professional association of prophets. He has not even been trained in the job, but is a herdsman (14, note present tense). Then he said, 'God took me and said, "Go, prophesy."' It is precisely the same divine calling, the same God-given message, which is the mark of the true prophet from Deut. **18** on.

But the rest of Amos' message appears to run clean contrary to the promises of Deut. **18**. He foresees a time of famine, people searching despairingly for a word from the Lord and not being able to find it (**8**.11 f.). The people had silenced the prophets, ignored them, or scorned them (**2**.11 f.); so God would not let people hear any more. But does this mean that prophecy would cease and revelation come to an end? Surely not entirely. There were no qualifications set against Deut. **18**, and the emphasis in Amos is on a famine of *hearing* the word. Yet whether the prophets were silent, or the people unable to hear, the result would be the same—the people left with no basis for life and no sense of direction. It is tempting—and many have done it—to apply this prophecy of spiritual famine to our own day, which is similar in many ways to life at the time of Amos. But while a good deal of Amos' prophecy is strikingly relevant, **8**.11 f. have to be seen in the light of Joel's foretelling of a new era of prophecy.

18 : Prophecy Regained

Joel 2.21–29

'Are we also among the prophets?' Dr. A. R. Vidler once put that question to present-day Christians, and he commented: 'The fact that the words "prophecy" and "prophet" have not been associated with anything in the living and constant experience of the great churches of Christendom or with normal features of the Christian life does not of course mean that there have in reality been no prophecy and prophets in the successive periods of church history. But I do suggest that the neglect not only of the words, but of explicit recognition of the gifts and endowments which they denote, has been a grave source of loss to the church.' Joel's prophecy was that the Spirit of God would be poured out on all flesh, and sons and daughters would all prophesy (28).

There is no doubt that the first part of this prophecy has been fulfilled. God's Spirit has been poured out. These are the latter days. Every Christian has received the gift of the Spirit. Peter's use of the prophecy of Joel (Acts **2**.17–21) and his offer of the gift of the Spirit (Acts **2**.38 f.) place that part of the prophecy, and the meaning of the phrase, 'on all flesh' (28), beyond doubt. But what of the gift of prophecy? And what are we to make of the inclusion of 'prophets' in the lists of spiritual gifts (1 Cor. **12**.10; Eph. **4**.11)?

It may be understood in two ways. One is to recognize that the essence of the prophetic gift is—in Jeremiah's word—a seat in God's council. This intimate fellowship with God, through the Spirit, was once the privilege of a select few. Now it is given to all. The longing Moses expressed has been fulfilled (Num. **11**.29). God has poured out His Spirit upon all. There is no longer any need for a go-between to bring God's word to man; all the Lord's people are prophets.

What then of the special gift which is indicated in 1 Cor. **12** and Eph. **4**, the gift which Agabus and Philip's four unmarried daughters exercised (Acts **11**.28; **21**.9–11)? Some maintain that there is evidence of the gift only in the first four centuries of the Christian Church, others that the gift is still exercised today. The central question concerns the nature of the gift. It may be visions and revelations (cf. 2 Cor. **12**.1–10); foreseeing future events (Acts **11**.28); understanding and expressing Christian truth with unusual clarity (1 Cor. **13**.2); or, as J. V. Taylor suggests, 'deliberate involvement in movements for peace, for civil rights, for integration and in action to deal with neighbourhood needs', a suggestion which is in line with the prophetic gift in the O.T.

The gift is not 'recognized' in the Church today in the way Dr. Vidler seems to suggest; would such recognition help? Since all the Lord's people are prophets, it is difficult to believe that God has withdrawn from His Church all four ways in which the special prophetic gift might be exercised.

For meditation : Romans ***12****.6.*

Questions and themes for study and discussion on Studies 14–18

1. How does the test of a true prophet (Deut. **18**.22) apply to Christ (Luke **7**.16)? Has this test of prophecy any relevance today?

2. Has Acts **2**.38, the gift of the Spirit, in any way altered Jer. **23**.22, the need to stand in God's council?
3. What is the evidence for and against the continued existence of the gift of prophecy in the Church today?

CHARACTER STUDIES

19 : Noah, who Obeyed God

Genesis 6.9–8.19

In one of his essays Montaigne remarked: 'The first law that ever God gave to man was a law of obedience, a commandment pure and simple, wherein man had nothing to enquire after or to dispute, forasmuch as to obey is the proper office of a rational soul acknowledging a heavenly benefactor.'

The memory of the first command, and what had flowed from its flouting by their first parents, must have been a firm tradition with Adam's posterity, passed, after the ancient fashion, from mouth to mouth, and inculcated in each succeeding generation. It is evident that in Noah the tradition held fast, for plain obedience is the hall-mark of his character.

The Euphrates plain was no stranger to floods. The flat river-valley drains a vast watershed of mountains, and archaeology finds abundant evidence of floods. The inundation of God's judgement, which was part of a warning and a command which came to Noah, was, however, something beyond all human experience. Noah was in the line of Enoch. He, too, 'walked with God' (6.9), and was blameless in God's sight. It is in such uncluttered hearts that awareness and conviction of God's will and purposes can grow.

Noah was called, by faith, to prepare. The great chapter on faith in Hebrews sets him thus in the lineage of his two great ancestors (Heb. 11.4–7). Abraham was to be the next in the noble line. The ark was no doubt long in building. No one else heeded the warning. Noah had his carpenters and shipwrights, for the project was far beyond the resources of one family. He was, it seems, an influential chief, for the gathering of ship-timber from remote forests for the task in the almost treeless plain must have been a vast undertaking. Noah must have incurred ridicule, but faith implies obedience, as the writer to the Hebrews continually stresses. Steadfastly he continued. There was some virtue in the huge preoccupations of the work. 'Doing the will of God leaves me no time for disputing about His plans,' said George Macdonald, and Noah had little time to question the still cloudless sky, and the continuing evidence that the carefree and corrupt society about him was right. He had been told to build. He obeyed. Obedience, first-fruit of trust, must have been an habitual part of him, for how true it is that obedience is not truly performed by the body, if the heart is dissatisfied.

20 : Noah's Lapse

Genesis 9

Faith was the mark of Noah's character, and it had new testings to endure. 'God remembered Noah,' says a revealing verse (8.1), and the words are full of meaning. Alone on the wide waters, with all the world they had known drowned and destroyed beneath them, the survivors must have endured anxiety and utter loneliness. No hint is given in the story of what went on in Noah's mind, but his faith is still apparent. Had God forgotten him? The question could have been a strong insistent one. He releases the raven and then the dove, putting thus a symbol of peace into the imagery and vocabulary of mankind. In due course faith found that for which it looked—the dry land, a new life, and a renewed covenant with God.

Then came Noah's strange lapse. The man who had earned a place in the honour roll of the faithful is seen drunk on the floor of his tent. We could well have been spared this picture, but the Bible is impartially frank in its revelation of the truth about the men and women who made its story. Perhaps there are circumstances unknown to us, as there always are in any spectacular demonstration of human failure. Tensions, sadness, joy, we might speculate endlessly concerning what lay behind Noah's excess. We do not know.

But look at the sorry situation without such speculation. Here was a good man defeated, a sight of shame which brought out the coarseness of one of his sons, and the delicacy and honour of the other two. Noah had lived through years of tension, over which his faith had triumphed. He failed and fell, like Elijah, in a moment of victory. Perhaps, indeed, the hour of triumph, when the long-borne burden is suddenly lifted, is the time of most dangerous assault. The mind relaxes from its long guard, and evil finds a new chink in the armour. So it was with Noah, and the curse on Canaan does nothing to enhance Noah in our eyes. He was called to suffer for Ham's conduct, and Ham may indeed have proved himself unworthy of trust, but the sad fact remains that Noah's carnality provided the context and occasion for Ham's sin. Let us pray that we may end well.

21 : Abraham of Ur

Hebrews 11.8–22

Environment and heredity both play their part in forming the character of a man, and of Abraham's environment we know a great deal. Of his ancestry, and its contribution to the shaping of one of the great men of all time, we know very little. Joshua (Josh. **24**.2) described Terah, Abraham's father, as a pagan, and his name seems to be connected with that of the moon-goddess, who was worshipped at Ur. This may mean very little, and Ur was no congenial dwelling-place for Terah, or he would not have so readily abandoned it with his son. But Terah's influence, by relationship or instruction, upon Abraham can only be a subject of speculation.

The port of Ur, however, and what it signified to its lively inhabitants, is closer to our knowledge. The ruins are not far from the confluence of the two great Mesopotamian rivers, and four millennia of river silt have built a plain which now separates Ur from the Sea by many miles. Harbour-works may be identified in the ruins of the town, and in ancient times it was obviously the gateway to the Middle East, and therefore to the caravan routes which wound up the Euphrates, curved round what is called the Fertile Crescent to Damascus, and down to the other river-valley civilization, that of Egypt on the Nile. And Egypt's delta looked to the Mediterranean where sailed the ships of Caphtor, Minoan Crete, and other cultures of prehistoric Europe.

Looking East, Ur faced the sealanes of the Persian Gulf, where man first learned to sail the high seas. The dhows coasted to the third of the river civilizations, that of the Indus Valley, where, in the ruins of the amazingly modern town of Mohenjo-Daro, pottery remains from Ur have been found. The traders doubtless penetrated much further east and touched Taprobane or Ceylon. There they met the junks from China and made contact with all the complex of Far Eastern trade.

Ur lay at the very centre of this vast web of human activity. It was a stimulating place for a man of intellect. Nowhere, more than at this nodal point of the ancient world's communications, could a man gain a greater and more detailed knowledge of the inhabited globe. From Crete, to Egypt, to Syria, and east to India and the Indies the long chain of Abraham's information stretched. It proved a mighty challenge.

22 : Abraham and God

Genesis 12.1–3; Acts 7.1–8

God prepares the heart and mind of man for His self-revelation. As he surveyed the wide world from his unique vantage-point, Abraham must have found one thought obtrusive. Ur, with its corrupt and idolatrous worship, was no exception. The world was lost in degrading views of God. From the bull-worship of Crete, to the animal deities of brilliant Egypt, from the worship of the Sun-god on the Phoenician coast, to the sadistic and sensual deities of which the sailors who traded to the Indus and the Malabar coast could tell, it was one wide story of burdensome corruption.

Some search for something purer, better, holier must have stirred in the heart of Abraham of Ur, because, at his first entrance on the story, he is described as knowing God (**12.1**). God meets those who seek Him, grants His grace to out-reaching faith, and speaks to those who listen (Acts **17**.26–28).

Abraham, brooding over benighted mankind, had found the only God. That discovery inspired, as it always will and must, a longing to share the saving and sanctifying truth.

All this must have taken place before Abraham appears in the Bible story. The great man knew, as few others in his age knew, the far-flung mass of humankind. His yearning, like his knowledge, must have embraced them all. He was the first man with the missionary urge within him. How could he impart the tremendous truth, which had become clear to him, to an audience so vast? He knew how long it took to ride on camel-back, or sail on shipboard, to the scattered nations of whose existence and need he had become aware. He knew that no one man could reach them all, and no one generation see their enlightenment.

But what if a nation could be founded, away from the corrupt centres of man, in the clean wilderness, a nation dedicated to the One God, and prepared to be the custodian and propagator of His truth? That is the vision in which the Hebrew nation began. God had moved in a questing and willing heart. God had prompted and led. A great soul had sought, heard, found and followed. That is perhaps how the call came to rise and march. So 'the glory of God appeared', as Stephen told the Sanhedrin, 'to Abraham, when he was in Mesopotamia, before he dwelt in Haran'.

23 : Abraham's Father

Joshua 24.1–5

At this point it might be profitable to return briefly to Terah, whose enigmatic person must be, as was earlier remarked, a matter of speculation only. There are, however, one or two pointers to reality. Stephen, in his historic address to the Sanhedrin, says quite clearly that the call to migrate and to found a people in the wilderness came not to the father, Terah, but to his son, Abraham, while the family still lived at Ur—a point not made clear in Genesis. Joshua speaks of the clan as worshippers of alien gods.

The picture which seems to emerge is that of a patriarchal

clan, with major acts of policy still firmly in the hands of the chief, Terah, but with large trust and acceptance given to his eldest son, Abraham. Conviction lays hold of the son, and a clear call comes to leave Ur, and its corruptions. For no other motive, perhaps, than his respect for his son's deep convictions, the head of the family agrees to migrate, but is strongly enough in control to dictate a pause at Haran, the Carrhae of Roman history, and the scene of the Parthians' spectacular victory over Crassus' three legions in 53 B.C.

Abraham was unwilling, in his father's lifetime, to oppose this pause in his fortunes. This was but limited obedience to the great call, and points to Terah's own limited understanding and faith. It was only after his father's death that Abraham felt free to move. In Gen. **12**.1 comes the call which Stephen says was clearly given in Ur. On Terah's death it was repeated, if the sequence of Gen. **11**.32; **12**.1 is chronological. It is more likely that the sequence is psychological, and that the two succeeding verses suggest a renewal of purpose, now that the impediment of Terah's imperfect faith was removed. It is thus that a father can muffle his son's call, impede his progress in the work of God, or, by his caution and unbelief, hold back the outworking of a divine plan in his son's life. Terah seems, as we peer back through history, to have been a man not without vision, not lacking a desire to abandon an inadequate life, or a corrupt environment, but for lack of bravery or conviction, to have fallen short of the best, and held his family back with him.

24 : Abraham's Retreat

Genesis 12.10–20

In Gen. **14**.13 there is a curious phrase—'Abraham the Hebrew'. The word appears to mean 'the Wanderer', the person who, in the modern world, is called 'the stateless man'. Read again the tribute in Heb. **11**. Abraham had left the environment which denied him his life's purpose, but he had left it at some cost. Terah had revealed, and Lot was to repeat the demonstration, that attachment to city life was strong in the tribe. Abraham left his city, and those who could not share his faith. And now Haran, like Ur, lay over the rim of the desert. Terah was dead, and however much the son may have deplored the father's tardiness, these were patriarchal days, and Abraham must have felt alone, and found the load of his responsibility heavy.

That, perhaps, is why caution overwhelmed faith at the first impact of famine. Abraham withdrew to Egypt, where the regular flooding of the Nile, fed by the vast reservoirs of the interior, protected agriculture, for the most part, from the effects of drought, disastrous in more exposed lands. Faith, in thoughtful and sensitive minds, is ever dogged by doubt. Thus it grows, in strife and contest. As Tennyson put it in his *In Memoriam* (*XCVI*):

'He fought his doubts and gathered strength,
He would not make his judgement blind.
He faced the spectres of the mind
And laid them; thus he came at length
To find a stronger faith his own . . .'

But such final victory is not always won in a single fight. Abraham knew defeat. He retreated to a land as corrupt as that which he had left, and ran straight into its pollution. Sarai, his wife, was the first to confront the peril. Abraham's half-truth—for Sarai was, in fact, a half-sister—reveals the dilemmas into which a man runs when he leaves the circle of God's will. He lied, and was rebuked by a pagan. Perhaps, too, it was in the course of this deviant adventure that Sarai acquired Hagar, her Egyptian maid, and set in motion those events which, linked each to each, were to influence Abraham's whole life and heritage, and to extend down through posterity to today's headlines. It is impossible, as Macbeth remarked, 'with the deed to trammel up the consequences'. Abraham was what Virgil called 'a hinge of fate'. Great events turned on him. None of us knows when we may be called to assume such a role. Faith treads valiantly and carefully.

25 : Abraham's Return

Genesis 13.1–7; Romans 4.1–8

No doubt chastened and relieved, Abraham passed through the barren Negev, and came to the place 'where his altar was in the beginning'. Here he 'called on the name of the Lord' (4). This, surely, is restoration. He had passed through a period of barrenness and alienation. His vision was dim. It is not impossible that his wife's continued childlessness was already beginning to impose some strain upon his faith, and to make his mighty concept of a people of God appear a little absurd. It all depended upon a simple sequence, the birth of an heir. Deepening anxiety on this score had played, perhaps, a part in the lapse of faith which had taken him to Egypt. There his very consciousness of God had dimmed.

The danger from which Sarai had been so wonderfully rescued, and the consequent peril to the purity of his whole eagerly desired line, may have awakened Abraham to the reality of God's continuing care, and called him to re-dedication. He traced his long path back to the sacred spot of his first worship in the land which had been promised to him, and in a new act of committal sought again the freshness of his faith.

It is a common enough experience in life to find each new act of faith and surrender challenged. No sooner had his heart been set right with God, than a fresh testing confronted him—strife in his own clan. Abraham's nephew Lot, since Terah's death, may have functioned as the deputy sheikh of the desert tribe. They had prospered in men and cattle. The limited grazing lands of the hill country, to which the sedentary city populations of the coastal plain and the Jordan valley tended to confine them, were inadequate for the common grazing of their herds and flocks. Strife broke out as strife does where human beings, eager for their own rights and advantage, are pressed too closely upon each other.

The final verse is significant. The alien dwelt in the land, and the words must mean that Abraham was jealous for the integrity of his tribe and its testimony before the corrupt society which was so closely observing him. He had found anew his peace with God. He was anxious now not to dishonour God by a spectacle of disunity and conflict within the group which had professed a new and greater loyalty to a God so different from the pagan deities worshipped commonly about them.

26 : Abraham's Faith

Genesis 13.8–18

Determined that there was to be no strife in the family of God, Abraham gave Lot the choice of dwelling-place. He had learned a deep lesson of faith in Egypt, and now he left the whole matter in the hands of God, though, in truth, as the patriarch, it was in his right to decide (Phil. **2**.5–8). The two chiefs stood on some eminence on the mountain spine of Palestine, from which the whole Jordan plain was visible. That deep rift valley runs down to the steaming Dead Sea, whose southern end appears today to cover the sites of Sodom and Gomorrah. Its seventy-mile length is traversed by the Jordan, whose convolutions make a stream almost four times as long as the river plain through which it winds its tortuous way. Lush tropical vegetation filled it (10) before the great eruption, which collapsed the southern end of the valley bottom, and spoiled some of the rich wealth of the long plain.

Set against this was the gaunt wilderness of the Judean uplands. From the point of view of material advantage, and human social contact, the choice for a worldly-minded man was quite obviously the Jordan valley. The wilderness held only loneliness, the harsh living of shepherds, the daily search for meagre pasture in the more sheltered vales, and all the stern testings of adverse environment of which Abraham was as aware as Lot. And yet Abraham, in quiet and sublime faith, allowed Lot to choose. Lot chose, and went his way. He 'moved his tent as far as Sodom' (12).

Observe now the pattern, setting these eleven verses side by side with those which told of Abraham's descent to Egypt, in search of those same advantages as Lot sought, as he moved towards the fertile and comfortable haunts of men. Moral peril quickly followed the great man's mistake, as it was to follow his nephew's similar error. But now Abraham had chosen the wise course, and left the outcome in the hands of God. After Lot had gone his way, God spoke to Abraham. From the high country of his camp, the length and breadth of the land was visible, from distant segments of the Mediterranean, to the blue walls of the Moab hills, from the far skylines which masked Galilee, to the southern haze where the Negev desert lay. This, said the Voice, was to be his land. Abraham built an altar near Hebron to remind himself of the covenant renewed.

Questions and themes for study and discussion on Studies 19–26

1. Define obedience. Is it reasonable?
2. What does Noah teach of parenthood?
3. How does environment shape character?
4. How is doubt best dealt with?
5. Look up Heb. **11**.1 in various translations, and define faith.
6. How is faith commonly tested? Illustrate from the Psalms.
7. How does the pursuit of material advantage corrupt faith?
8. How do we still 'build an altar'?

THE GOD WHO SPEAKS

The God who Speaks—in Christ

27 : The Word of God

John 1.1–18

The Prologue to John's Gospel is like one of the world's richest diamond mines. Some choice jewels have long been in circulation, brilliantly polished and of incalculable value; fresh discoveries are continually being made; and yet there are still rich resources to be mined.

Most commentaries and study guides find the Prologue so full and suggestive that they take it as several substantial readings, but there is also considerable advantage in deliberately trying to see the picture whole, concentrating on the movement of thought from v. 1 to v. 18. It may be, as many suggest, that various separate strands of thought have been woven into the whole, but there is still a marvellous and significant unity of thought.

The dominant theme is that God speaks. He makes Himself known to man. The opening verses are packed with the key words of revelation—Word, life, light, testimony, witness (1–8); the same is true of the closing verses (14–18). The Prologue as a whole sets out in a chronological framework the full plan of revelation—the historical events and their theological significance. It begins before time, like Gen. 1.1 which it echoes, and it begins with God. 'God's self-disclosure was implicit in the being of God Himself (1). God was never without self-expression' (C. K. Barrett). The world exists, because it is the nature of God to communicate Himself (3);

the life of God is the life and the light of men (4). At v. 5, the stage is set for God's direct intervention. The coming of John is an indispensable witness to the final, complete word of revelation, the appearance of God Himself on the stage of history (6–8), in the life and ministry of Christ. For some at least, this leads to the climax of revelation, new birth by the direct action and will of God (13).

Verse 14 is not the climax of the Prologue; it is a striking repetition of vs. 9–11, and is intended to continue and develop the theme. The word 'beheld' (past tense) refers to the ministry, in which the glory of God was seen; for John, humble, sacrificial love, full of grace and truth, is glory. The witness of the Baptist to the pre-eminence of Christ has been fulfilled (15, which ought not to be in brackets); the continuing evidence of His supremacy is in the grace, the generosity, with which He gives one gift after another to His children (16). John defines grace by contrast with the partial revelation through Moses and the law. In Christ, revelation is complete—it is 'grace and truth' (17). In Christ, God has shown to men everything they need to know. The Prologue began with God revealing Himself to man. It ends with the revelation complete.

For meditation: 'Could anything be more glorious than to have so much to give, and give it all?' (*M. Irwin*).

28 : God's Word and Christ's Ministry

Luke 4.16–37

The trouble at Nazareth was that they knew Him too well. The reputation of the young Galilean preacher had spread fast (14), and the people of His home town were glad to welcome Him again. Of course, He was invited to preach; and His words, which should have rocked them back on their heels in stupefied silence, aroused only patronizing admiration (22). Jesus had taken a most significant passage of Scripture, Isa. 61.1 f., and had claimed that the things He was doing, of which they had heard reports, were a direct fulfilment of it (21). It was an astonishing claim, but His own people missed it altogether. They were too busy congratulating themselves on having produced such a good local preacher. Then it all turned sour on them. Jesus had stopped short in His quotation from Isaiah; the next words are 'and the day of vengeance of our God' (Isa. **61**.2), which were understood to mean salvation for Israel but vengeance for everyone else. In the rest of His sermon, Jesus shows from the Scriptures that God's favour is no narrow, sectarian privilege to be possessed by one nation; it embraces all (23–27). It was a further explanation of the missionary charter He had taken up in vs. 18 f., with the four main thrusts which characterized His ministry—evangelism, social action, healing and prophecy.

The second congregation, at Capernaum, was astonished at His authority (32) and amazed at His power (36). Their reaction in v. 36 is highly significant if seen in the light of John **1**, not 'Who is this?' but 'What is this word?' They were beginning to realize what the evil spirit had instantly perceived (34, cf. v. 41), that God Himself was speaking directly to men through Christ. To the Jews, the words of ordinary men were more than sounds useful for communication; words had power to achieve results. How much more powerful was God's word! From Gen. **1** onwards (3, 6, 11), the Bible speaks of God's word as a dynamic force (Isa. **55**.11; Psa. **33**.8 f.). It is this understanding of 'word' which underlines the question the people of Capernaum asked about Christ and it is with the same understanding that we should study such phrases as 'the message (word) of this salvation' (Acts **13**.26), 'the word of life' (Phil. **2**.16), and 'the word of truth' (Eph. **1**.13), all of which stem from God's word in Christ.

29 : God's Word and Christ's Teaching

John 8.21–30

It is really no wonder that the Pharisees were baffled, frustrated, intrigued, and at times furiously angry with Christ. 'Who are you?' they ask, in despairing bewilderment (25). The reply Christ gives is as clear and straightforward as it could possibly be in the circumstances. Had He gone further and claimed to be God, He would have been instantly stoned (cf. John **10**.31–33).

The reply has four main points: Christ has been sent by God (26 f.), His message is from God, with God's full authority (26, 28), what He does and says is always pleasing to God (29), and the most convincing evidence of the truth of this would be given later (28). What Jesus says about the origin of His teaching is, at first sight, parallel to the phrase which occurs so frequently in the O.T. (3,808 times): 'The word of the Lord came to. . . .' But in the O.T., the prophets generally introduced their teaching with the words 'Thus saith the Lord'. Never once does Jesus use this phrase. He spoke as One who had authority. It was His 'Truly I say to you' which astonished the people (Matt. **7**.28 f.). The translation 'I do nothing on my own authority' (28), while it emphasizes that Jesus spoke with divine authority, may perhaps be confusing. It is literally 'I do nothing of myself' (cf. **5**.30–32). 'If He were to act independently of God (supposing such a thing to be possible) Jesus would be completely powerless. The whole meaning and energy of His work lie in the fact that it is not His work but God's' (C. K. Barrett). His words and His works arise directly out of the deepest possible relationship to the Father, and they therefore reveal the truth of God (26). They are grounded in what William Temple describes as 'this simple claim to divine companionship' (29). On the result of the teaching (30), Temple comments: 'So it always is. When a Christian can say that he has Christ in his heart, and offers a practical obedience as evidence and ground of this, he too wins many for his Lord.'

30 : Christ—the Heart of God's Word

Acts 2.22–39

It is difficult, perhaps impossible, for a Christian of today to imagine himself in Jerusalem, watching and listening as the disciples tumble out on to the streets on the day of Pentecost. The things Peter and the disciples said about the cruelly evil and so recent execution of their Master are so staggering that their first shocking impact can hardly be recaptured. Some oft-quoted words of D. M. Baillie are worth pondering: 'The crucifixion of Jesus set men thinking more than anything else that has ever happened in the life of the human race. And the most remarkable fact in the whole history of religious thought is this: that when the early Christians looked back and pondered on the dreadful thing that had happened, it made them think of the redeeming love of God. Not simply of the love of Jesus, but of the love of God.'

Peter proclaims 'Jesus the Nazarene' as a man whose credentials, 'mighty works, wonders and signs', were clearly divine. His hearers knew this (cf. Luke **7**.16; **24**.19; John **6**.14); they had seen it for themselves. They also knew that He had been executed, and they thought, therefore, that He had died under God's curse (Gal. **3**.13). What Peter tells them is, astonishingly, the exact opposite (23). The crucifixion was the will of God. Even though the men who allowed themselves to be responsible for it were 'lawless' evil men, the cross was God's 'definite plan' (cf. **3**.18). 'But God raised him' means, from a human point of view, that a tragedy has been turned into a triumph. In terms of God's plan, it means that the revelation is complete and the work of redemption done. The cross alone was half a sentence, a nonsense arousing only despair. The full sentence is clear, true and glorious.

The importance of v. 23, and the depth of meaning in it, may be seen in two other N.T. passages. In Rom. **5**.6, Paul talks about Christ's death, and it might be expected that he would go on to speak of this as proof of Christ's love. In fact, he speaks in v. 8 of the death of Christ as the revelation of God's love. The other passage is John **12**.32 f. Peter says, in his speech in Acts **2**, that Christ is now *exalted* at the right hand of God (33). Exactly the same word is used in John **12**.32, 'lifted up', to describe the crucifixion. It means far more than physical movement; it indicates that the cross itself is the glory of God (cf. John **8**.28; **13**.31 f.). 'The act whereby Jesus is destroyed becomes . . . the final disclosure of the glory of God in the self-giving love which is victorious' (A. M. Ramsey).

31 : 'Seen and Heard'

1 John 1.1–2.6

(This study concentrates on vs. 1–4, and the next on **1**.5–**2**.6)

Like the Prologue to John's Gospel, the first chapter of 1 John summarizes the essential truth about God's revelation. The heart of God's word to man is the 'word of life' (1). He was 'from the beginning', a phrase which, as in John **1**.1–3, probably refers to the existence of Christ before time, rather than to the beginning of the ministry; now, that 'eternal life' has been 'made manifest to us' (2). The words emphasize that the revelation is a fact of history, a reality which has been 'heard', 'seen', and 'touched'. 'To have heard was not enough; men heard God's voice in the Old Testament. To have seen was more compelling. But to have handled was the conclusive proof of material reality, that the Word was "made flesh, and dwelt among us"' (Scott). Revelation is nothing less than God, who existed before all time, making it possible for men to touch Him.

The Greek verb translated 'we have seen with our eyes' (1) is different from the other verbs—'seen' (1) and 'saw' (2). It 'expresses the calm, intent, continuous contemplation of an object which remains before the spectator. . . . The first two verbs (heard, seen) express the fact, and the second two (looked upon, touched) the definite investigation by the observer' (Westcott).

The rather complicated grammar of vs. 1–3, with v. 2 in brackets and the opening words of v. 3 taking up the theme of v. 1, all leads up to the main verb, 'we proclaim' (3). The central fact of revelation, being a fact of history, must be passed on. In his notable book, 'The Founder of Christianity', C. H. Dodd emphasizes the critical importance of history for Christian faith: 'in these events of ancient time God was at work among men and it is from His action in history rather than from abstract arguments that we learn what God is like, and what are the principles on which He deals with men, now as always. The Church—every gathering of the Church, everywhere, under every form—*remembers* that on a certain night its Founder "suffered under Pontius Pilate". The Church remembers an event which is actual, concrete and in principle dateable like any other historical event'.

For meditation: 'The whole Christian life is a life of remembrance which issues in thanksgiving' (*J. Baillie*).

32 : 'This is the Message'

1 John 1.5–2.6

It is clear from vs. 1–4 that the heart of the Christian message is the 'word of life' who was seen and heard and intently watched. From the beginning, therefore, handing on the message was an act of memory; those who had seen and heard had to 'testify to it'. But as C. H. Dodd goes on to say, 'It was a memory now illuminated by a discovery that left them at first gasping with astonishment: that the Leader they had thought irretrïevably lost had got the better of death itself, in a way as inexplicable as it was indubitable.'

'Memory illuminated'—it is a significant phrase. The message handed on in **1**.5–**2**.6 is far more than basic historical fact; it is the facts plus their meaning. Both together have been 'heard from him' (**1**.5), that is, from Christ. The life Christ lived showed that God is light (**1**.5, cf. John **8**.12). The death He died was a death which 'cleanses us from all sin' (7, cf. Mark **10**.45). Revelation is God alive on earth in Christ, doing things and making it possible for men to understand His action.

The particular way in which the truth is put in **1**.5–**2**.2 is aimed at refuting false teaching. There were heretical teachers asserting either that men were without sin (8), or that men did not sin (10). They maintained that it was possible to have fellowship with God and at the same time to walk in darkness (**1**.6). Against this, John sets the central importance of God's revelation in Christ (**2**.1 f.) and the unbreakable link between faith in Christ and obedience to His word (**2**.3–6). It would be possible to indulge in a theological 'chicken and egg' discourse on vs. 3 and 5; which comes first, assurance and then obedience, obedience and then love, or the other way round. Surely the truth is that a genuine Christian is on an upward spiral; obedience gives greater assurance, and assurance leads to obedience; to keep His word deepens love and deeper love becomes an incentive to obedience. The pattern, both of obedience and love, is Christ Himself (**2**.6, cf. Phil. **2**.8; John **15**.12–14).

Questions and themes for study and discussion on Studies 27–32

1. What is the meaning of the description of Jesus as 'the Word of God'?
2. In Christ's ministry, what was the relation between preaching and healing?
3. What is the significance, for our presentation of the gospel, of the N.T. connection between events and their meaning?

CHARACTER STUDIES

33 : Lot

Luke 17.22–32

We may pause for a moment to look down the river plain and consider Lot. Faith sets the future above the present, the unseen above the seen, God's will above all things. Lot had not done this. Why? 'Living in tents' (Heb. **11**.9) had been hard. Had the sojourn in Egypt given the family a renewed taste for city life? Where to locate one's family is sometimes an important question in a parent's endeavour to ensure their salvation.

And did Lot, having observed Abraham's own long frustration under Terah, think that, in terms of his own personal honour and advantage, a subordinate post under the patriarch had little to offer? He became a judge in Sodom, and the fact may be a glimpse of unexpressed ambitions (Gen. **19**.1; 'to sit in the gate' was a technical expression for a judge). The city in the plain seemed to offer much to 'the lust of the eyes', for it was the old temptation over again, pressing hard on a character which did not look for a 'city without foundations'. The unseen, which Lot did not consider, was shocking —the corruption beneath the bright surface of Sodom's wealth, and the sure judgement of God upon its sin, and upon those who shared its sin. He could not see that a prayerless, hasty, carnal choice was destined to lead to the death of his wife, the loss of his possessions, the corruption of his family, and the foundation of a pagan posterity. We should beware of what we choose.

We saw two men standing at the place of decision. Such

moments, like some persistent eddy in a stream, come in life, and determine its texture. There is a dual tug—the eternal pull of evil, and the eternal pull of God's spirit. As James Russell Lowell put it:

Once to every man and nation comes the moment
to decide,
In the strife of Truth and Falsehood, for the good
or evil side;
Some great cause, God's new Messiah, offering each
the bloom or blight,
Parts the goats upon the left hand, and the sheep
upon the right,
And the choice goes by forever 'twixt that darkness
and that light.

We never know amid the flow of life's choices, which will be final and irreversible. The 'great cause' which faced the two men on the hill-top was the founding of a nation for God. They both chose and the moment passed. So men seal their destiny.

34 : Abraham's Raid

Genesis 14.1–16; 2 Corinthians 6.11–18

The story of Abraham's rescue of Lot breaks unexpectedly into the narrative. The reader hardly expects to meet the patriarch in the role of desert guerrilla fighter. It was a task thrust upon him. A small confederation of chiefs from the Euphrates valley had sent a punitive expedition down to Sodom, and had sacked the plain. Lot shared the misfortune of his associates.

The story must have come from Abraham, who, it may be guessed, was careful to preserve the records of a family on which such a destiny rested. If so, we must ascribe the brevity of a notable historical document to the modesty of the writer, who saw the hand of God in a victory so complete.

Abraham's decision and initiative, none the less, and the strength of his growing household, show clearly in the story (14). His men knew all the paths and byways of the wilderness, and the forces from the north were no doubt as prone to panic as Eastern armies were. They had, in fact, good reason to be afraid. Palestine was an Egyptian sphere of influence. The Nile empire, through all her history and on to the present day, has regarded the narrow land to the north of her as a buffer against the powers which, from the Hittites to Persia, constituted a threat to Egyptian security. At the same time, Egypt seldom held more than the long coastal plain with any vigour or completeness. Hence the possibility of petty war and raiding in the hilly hinterland, a border plague which even the Romans found it difficult to control.

Raiding parties like the one in the story would risk an inroad, but would be anxious to retreat into the desert, and would be in some apprehension of pursuit. For all they knew, any attack from behind them could only be a task-force of the Egyptians. Hence the rapid success of Abraham's well-planned, and sudden night-attack, and the impunity of his withdrawal.

Lot was saved by the bold and competent leadership of the uncle whom he had abandoned, and restored to his chosen environment without reproach. The fact that, after a lesson so sharp, he returned to Sodom, is indication enough of how deeply the life he had adopted had penetrated him. Faith, observe, is not quietism. In this story Abraham acts with the speed of a Bedu raider.

35 : Abraham's Friend

Genesis 14.17–20; Hebrews 7.1–10

Melchizedek, king of Salem, is an intriguing person. Like Moses' princess, he steps with dignity into half a page of Bible history, and then is gone. His significance, however, is out of all proportion to the amount of space his story fills. He came down from the hills when Abraham returned from his night raid, heavy with the spoils of Sodom, then stepped back out of the story, leaving us hungry to know him. His character left a deep impression, for the writer of Psa. **110** and the writer of the Epistle to the Hebrews found him a fascinating figure of Christ.

Psa. **110** looks forward to one who combines the offices of king and priest, but a priest of no common order, apart from the line of Aaron. Preoccupied as he was with the O.T., the writer of Hebrews also finds the mysterious priest of Genesis significant. As the first chapter of the epistle shows (1.3), Psa. **110** was prominent in the author's mind, and in Chs. **5-7** he expounds his difficult theme of one who foreshadowed the Lord before Aaron. Aaron's priesthood and the law.

Archaeology has something to say on the theme. The passage in Hebrews says that Melchizedek was 'without father and mother', which simply means that he founded his dynasty. It was also a 'king of Salem', who boasts in the famous Tell-el-Amarna letters of 1380 B.C.: Behold this land, neither my father nor my mother gave it me—the hand of the mighty King gave it me.' The words explain the text from Hebrews.

Archaeology can thus, strangely enough, produce another person not dissimilar to the good priest-king of Salem. It emerges that, although the Bible speaks of the line of revelation which found consummation in Christ, the truth was known and cherished elsewhere. Perhaps there lies in the fact some anticipation of the universal gospel which Paul was to preach.

36 : Abraham and the King of Sodom

Genesis 14.21–24

We lingered over the most puzzling character in *Genesis*, Melchizedek of Jerusalem, because it is evident that Abraham recognized his superiority. This chapter is rich in facets of the patriarch's character. We noted his modesty, his firm decisiveness and action in face of crisis, his graciousness towards erring Lot, his humility and courtesy to the stately king . . . Observe now his upright determination to be separate from unclean gain (23).

Sodom was sunk in the corruption which put a base word into the languages of the world. People generally get the rulers they deserve, and the ruler of Sodom, no doubt, reflected the vices which he permitted or was powerless to prevent, in the community he governed. Abraham revealed something of the man's character when he mentioned, with a touch of irony, the peril he was eager to shun. He did not wish to hear, in the gossip of the land, that 'the king of Sodom made Abraham rich'.

Perhaps this was a reflection of talk commonly heard about Lot, who had demeaned himself to accept the hospitality of Sodom, and the honour of office at their hands. In a corrupt society such boons are too often conferred in the hope that the recipient will be compromised, and Sodom must have regarded their sojourner from the increasingly powerful desert tribe, a worthwhile asset. Indeed the events of the raid clearly demonstrated the fact. But for the guerrilla campaign of the shepherds, Sodom would have remained stripped and forlorn.

Abraham wanted no compromising alliance. When he left Ur and Haran, and retired from the ill-starred expedition into Egypt, Abraham had divested himself of the urban entanglements which might have compromised his plan for a clean society. He had conferred a boon on the ungodly, but wanted to be under no obligation to them. Observe how he was inspired and aided in this wise and upright decision. He met the good Melchizedek, and was able to view the man of Sodom side by side with the man of Jerusalem. To meet good men and women on the Lord's day often aids us when we are confronted with a lesser world throughout the week. To commune with Christ every morning, is to steady mind and heart when we meet, in the rush and press of life, those who will have none of Him. But note that history was outworking through Abraham, faulty but faithful, not through the statuesque king of Salem.

37 : Reaction

Genesis 15

'Courage,' said Plutarch, 'consists not in hazarding without fear, but being resolutely minded in a just cause.' Abraham had demonstrated this when, with his band of young men, he attacked an army. But in the weariness which follows resolute action there is sometimes a rebound, and sudden fear. We see Elijah, at the peak of his brave career, succumb to that sudden and most human reaction. And so did Abraham.

It was probably the following night, and it is in night's murk and loneliness that courage most commonly ebbs. With the need for action over, and time to think, Abraham began to fear that courage had been rashness, and swift valour foolhardiness. He could well imagine what the raiders from the river would think and do when full day dawned and they recovered from their panic-stricken flight. A fast reconnaissance on camel-back would establish the fact that there was no regular Egyptian force in the vicinity. The desert nomads are uncanny in their ability to read the signs in the sand, and it is likely enough that the size and nature of the attacking guerrilla-force were plain for skilled trackers' eyes to assess.

Abraham would imagine all this and pass on to the dire conclusion that, by the middle of the day, his enemies would know who had attacked them, and where he lived. Then would come the revengeful raid. And it was all for back-slidden Lot. Then, too, he might continue, in the sick reasonings of the night, was it common sense to rebuff the ruler of Sodom in the exaltation which followed the conversation with the saintly Melchizedek?

At which, clear in Abraham's inner being, came the voice which he had learned to recognize as the voice of his God: 'Fear not, Abram, I am your shield; your reward shall be very great.'

With a great surge of faith renewed, the patriarch, calmed now and at peace, went out into the night. The cold sand was under his feet, the stars shone in uncovered splendour in the chill night (5). So should his offspring be—and v. 6 put a great text into the Bible.

38 : Abraham and Hagar

Genesis 16

The events of this chapter were as repugnant to later ideas of the Hebrews as they are to us, but they conformed to the Code of Hammurabi, and to laws familiar to Abraham in Ur and Haran. Two relevant provisions, both of which Sarai had in mind, run: 'If a man marries a wife, and she has not given him children, if that man marries his concubine and brings her into his house, then that concubine shall not rank with his wife.' And again: 'If a man has married a wife, and she has given her husband a female slave who bears him children, and afterwards that slave ranks herself with her mistress, because she has borne children, her mistress shall not sell her for silver . . . The concubine shall be fettered and counted among the slaves.' From which provisions it appears that, in the terms of the secular law, Sarai did not treat Hagar as harshly as she was permitted to do.

It is, however, at the personalities of the story that we are looking principally, and the question arises why Abraham had recourse to a secular and pagan law, when he found himself still without an heir. Sarai may have marked and pitied his anxiety, for he had staked his whole life on this venture of faith. He had, at great sacrifice, and at the cost of lonely exile, provided an unencumbered environment for his posterity—but what if posterity were denied him?

It was without doubt a failure of a sorely tried faith which persuaded Abraham to descend to this permitted subterfuge—a failure perhaps aided by a breath of carnality of the sort to which the flesh is prone. Abraham was not perfect, and it is important to remember Paul's insistent emphasis on the fact that he was not perfect. He was a fallible man but he believed God, and that was counted to him for righteousness. And whose faith is perfect? Faith grows with the assaults upon it. Doubt dogs its exercise, and the great patriarch was no exception. But no such mistake goes without its consequences. The line of Ishmael still opposes Isaac and continues to multiply the pain one step of faithlessness can cause.

39 : Abraham and the Covenant

Genesis 17

We have called the patriarch by his common name throughout because it is under the nomenclature of the Abrahamic Covenant that he is known in the New Testament. Strictly, up to this point in the narrative, he was known as Abram. It is popularly believed that Abram means 'exalted father', and Abraham 'father of a multitude', and these translations could be correct, but in actual fact the etymology of both names is far from certain. One point is sure, 'ab' signifies father, and it was only the birth of Ishmael which rescued either name from taunt and ridicule.

Hence the remark in v. 18, and the pathos embedded in it. The old promise, almost forgotten over the thirteen years since the stormy events of Ishmael's birth, was convincingly renewed. But Abraham was old, and the covenant proposed seemed more and more to mock his virtually childless state. He clung with some desperation to the one chance of posterity, the son of the Egyptian servant-girl. 'Oh that Ishmael might live in thy sight', is a yearning prayer to have done with testing and further waiting, and to have the one son born to him, for all the blemish on the lineage, declared the heir. Such a promise would break the tension in which he lived.

It was natural enough. Time-bound man chafes at God's long delays. 'O Lord, make haste to help us' is the most human of man's prayers. And the Lord Himself permitted us, in the prayer which was given to be a model for all prayers, to ask to be delivered from temptation. It is not always God's will that we should be so delivered, and that is a theme Paul takes up in the first five verses of Rom. **5**. Abraham was establishing the pattern of saving faith. He did not know the part which he and his belief were to play in plans yet unrevealed for man, and among that other posterity which were to be 'as the stars of heaven'. There was purpose in God's delays, and Abraham, still puzzled and desperately perplexed, believed, and fulfilled the obligations of the new covenant made with him. It is a strong faith which continues to march when there is no light at all upon the way, and does not doubt in the darkness what God told when it was light.

40 : Abraham the Host

Genesis 18

'If a man be gracious to strangers, it shows that he is a citizen of the world,' said Francis Bacon, 'and that his heart is no island, cut off from other islands, but a continent that joins them.' Abraham was not embittered by the vast disappointment which, to this very date, had held his life in tension. In his human relationships he retained his Eastern courtesy and hospitality. 'Do not neglect to show hospitality to strangers,' runs a famous verse in Hebrews (**13**.1), 'for thereby some have entertained angels unawares.' The reference was to this scene. From his noonday rest in the door of his tent, Abraham was stirred to action by the arrival of strange and unrecognized guests. It was only with dawning insight that the patriarch realized that they were no ordinary messengers, and somehow succeeded in conveying to Sarah, in the seclusion of the tent, that the entertainment of that afternoon was no common experience. With a woman's live curiosity she was keenly listening, and heard words which surprised and embarrassed her.

But there was apprehension, too, as well as exultation in the great elusive promise renewed. The strangers rose, and set off towards Sodom, and Abraham heard the tale of coming catastrophe. There follows the moving story of intercessory prayer, which put a potent and consoling text into the speculation of man upon God's judgements, and the last things: 'Shall not the Judge of all the earth do right?' (25). Indeed He will—beyond our imagining, satisfying all our loftiest and most refined ideas of justice, with equity complete and overwhelming . . .

Abraham's line of thought is clear. Peter's testimony preserves an ancient tradition that Lot had not surrendered to the abominations of his environment (2 Pet. **2**.7). Abraham was aware of this, and for all the retreat of Lot, which he must have deplored, he must have been confident that the renegade had kept his household pure. Surely, in the small den of iniquity down on the plain, there was one island of righteous life? Ten was no doubt the number at which Abraham assessed the small urban household of his departed nephew. At that point he stopped praying. Here begins the doctrine of the Remnant, the 'salt of the earth', which from then till now has preserved corrupt societies from final disintegration.

Questions and themes for study and discussion on Studies 33–40

1. Trace the imagery of the shield through Scripture.

2. What has Hebrews to say of Melchizedek?
3. How can God be a reward? Consider Heb. **11**.6.
4. What is a 'covenant'?
5. What significance lies in a name in Hebrew belief?
6. What have you learned from the character of Abraham?
7. Consider the frankness of Scripture about human faults.

THE GOD WHO SPEAKS

The Jews, the Scriptures and the Messiah

41 : Delight in the Law

Psalm 119.129–144

A few moments' thought about the fuss there is today over laws, rules and authority, followed by another careful reading of Psa. **119**.129–144, makes an astonishing contrast. It would be easy to echo v. 136 and pray for a new spirit of submissiveness. Such phrases as 'thy commandments are my delight' (143) or 'thy law is true' (142) do not exactly capture the spirit of our own age. But we misunderstand altogether what is happening today if we label rebellious students and permissive yippies as 'anti-authority' and imagine we have solved everything. The fundamental problem is not authority and obedience, but reality and stability.

Psa. **119** is a psalm for our day. The psalmist's delight is not in obedient submission to a domineering authority but in the reality and stability of the law. In v. 142, the law is said to be true. It has been 'appointed in righteousness' (138). This means that the commandments of God are true in the sense that they are real, valid, stable. They hold together firmly. They are a solid, reliable foundation for life. And they are so because God Himself is true and righteous. Verse 137 is of crucial importance. The law is righteous because God is righteous. It is just because God is just. The Jews delighted in the law not because it was the authority to which they had to submit but because in the law they touched rock—the reality and eternal stability of God Himself. It was because of that fact that they described the law in terms which may seem to us extravagant.

If the law was 'detached' from the being of God Himself, and given an 'independent' authority, it quickly became either a means of self-righteousness or a crushing burden. For some of the Pharisees, the law was an opportunity for delight in their self-righteousness. In Paul, before his conversion, the law aroused despair. But for those who found in the law the truth of God Himself, it was 'sweeter than honey'.

Prayer : *'Lord, You are just indeed;*
Your decrees are right.
You have imposed Your will with justice
and with absolute truth.
The justice of Your will is eternal,
If You teach me, I shall live'
(Gelineau version).

42 : Inspired and Profitable

2 Timothy 3.10–17

Those Jewish children whose parents understood and appreciated the law, and avoided the perils of Pharisaism, were fortunate indeed. Timothy's mother and grandmother were people of sincere faith, which presumably means Christian faith (1.5), but they must have been teaching Timothy the truth of the Scriptures from a time well before their conversion (15, the Greek indicates 'from infancy'). It is of great significance that Paul, a Jewish Christian, gives Timothy strong encouragement to go on studying 'the sacred writings'. They are able 'to instruct you for salvation', in contrast to the corruptions of those 'who will listen to anybody and can never arrive at a knowledge of the truth' (7).

The phrase 'all scripture is inspired' has an alternative translation in the RSV margin, and different translations are grammatically possible. The balance of discussion favours the version in the RSV text, and emphasizes that the whole of Scripture—literally, every single part which goes to make up the whole—is both inspired and profitable.

In using the word 'inspired'—literally, 'breathed out by God'—Paul chose a word which 'accurately expresses the view of the inspiration of the O.T. prevalent among Jews of the first century. The church took it over entire' (J. N. D. Kelly). The word describes vividly the fact of the divine inspiration of Scripture but does not offer any particular theory about how God did it.

Of the four points mentioned to indicate how profitable the Scriptures are, two apparently refer to doctrines and two to conduct. Significantly, two are positive and two negative. There may be some truth in that over-worked modern motto, 'people are right in what they affirm and wrong in what they deny', but it is not the whole truth. If a statement is true, its opposite is untrue. The truth of Scripture is profitable for teaching; the opposite is not. Both teaching and reproof are necessary; correction as well as training in righteousness.

43 : Prophetic Inspiration

2 Peter 1.12–2.3

The Scriptures contain a great many direct statements and other indications of the fact that they are inspired, but the nearest the N.T. comes to a 'theory' of inspiration is in v. 20 f. Like Paul in 2 Timothy, Peter is writing as a Jewish Christian, expressing the understanding of inspiration current among first-century Jews. The 'theory' of inspiration—an indication, that is, of how God did it—is no more than a word in v. 21. Men were 'moved', which means 'carried along', by the Holy Spirit. The word refers to sailing ships. 'The prophets raised their sails, so to speak (they were obedient and receptive) and the Holy Spirit filled them and carried their craft along in the direction He wished' (E. M. B. Green).

This does not mean that the Holy Spirit 'took over' the personalities and mental processes of the prophets and apostles. It implies that He prepared the men, their backgrounds, experiences and circumstances, so that they wrote what God wanted them to write. They were 'holy men', dedicated to God, but also, for the most part, free men. Visions and trances were rare compared to the 'pressure of circumstances' through which God inspired such writing as Paul's letters.

There are many parallels in history to illustrate this 'process' of inspiration, though none to compare with its results. The plays of Shakespeare, for example, were not written by a man in a trance. According to G. M. Trevelyan, 'His work would never have been produced in any other period than those late Elizabethan and early Jacobean times in which it was his luck to live. He could not have written as he did, if the men and women among whom his days were passed had been other than they were, in habits of thought, life and speech, or if the London theatres in the years just after the Armada had not reached a certain stage of development, ready to his shaping hand.'

Apart from the teaching about inspiration, this passage contains two difficult but important questions of interpretation. In v. 20, the RSV may be misleading in 'one's own interpretation', which makes the verse refer to *our* understanding of Scripture. The Greek means literally 'private unravelling'; it may refer to the inspiration of the prophets themselves, who did not offer their own private views on events, 'because . . .' v. 21 (cf. Phillips).

In v. 19a, two interpretations are possible, neither clear from the RSV. Peter may be saying that the events he witnessed fulfilled and therefore confirmed the truth of prophecy; or that the prophetic word is a more reliable proof of the truth of events than his account. The latter is more consistent with Jewish views of the O.T. 'Since the Jews were in no doubt that everything that the prophets taught came from God, it is no wonder that Peter says that their word is more sure' (Calvin).

44 : Tradition versus Life

Mark 7.1–13

An irate father who wants to 'cut off his son with five new pence' has to *cancel* his will and make another; a Greek father would have had his will *made void*. The same word, used by Christ in v. 13, vividly describes the way in which the Pharisees and Sadducees *cancelled out* God's Word, and set their tradition in its place. Three times in a few verses,

Christ contrasts their traditions with the commandments of God (leave – hold fast, 8; reject – keep, 9; make void – hand on, 13). They talked about 'the tradition of the elders' (5), a phrase which implied an authority and status for tradition similar to that of the law itself; Christ spoke about the traditions of men (7 f.). More emphatic still is the contrast in vs. 10 f., 'Moses said . . . but you say'.

Such distinctions probably horrified the Pharisees. They thought that what Moses said and what they said were one and the same thing, that Scripture and tradition were identical. Over the years, the Jewish Rabbis had built up a formidable body of tradition which codified the law and set out in detail what could or could not be done in almost any situation. Ceremonial hand-washing was a case in point (1–5). Christ says nothing about its value, since it was not commanded in the law but nor was it in conflict with the law. He takes a more potent illustration. Keeping vows was specifically commanded in the law (cf. Num. **30**.1 f.); but the Pharisees, in their tradition, spelled out in detail the vows that could be made—such as promising money to God (11). They then realized that some vows might contradict other parts of the law, so they made judgements about priorities, wrong judgements (10–12), and made their tradition more important than God's Word.

How could people who recognized so clearly the authority and full inspiration of Scripture make such blunders? Christ's use in vs. 6 f. of the quotation from Isa. **29**.13 indicates that they respected the law but not the Giver of the law. They 'detached' the righteous law from the righteous God who gave it, and inevitably their understanding of it became unrighteous (cf. study of Psa. **119**.129–144). They did not serve the just God who gave the law, so inevitably they perverted the just law into injustice.

45 : God's Word or Man's

John 5.30–47

It was inevitable that Jews who exalted their own traditions above the Word of God should miss the central message of the Scriptures. The cause of the injustice which Christ rebuked in Mark **7** is clearly set out in John 5.39. The word 'search' indicates meticulous scrutiny, close attention to every detail. It suggests the critical approach of a person who will examine a great painting at close quarters to make sure the forms and textures are correct, rather than the admiring gaze of the person who stands back and sees the beauty and colour and design of the whole. The word 'in' is also significant, indicating that they tried to find life in what had been given rather than in the Giver. 'You' in '*you* think that in them you have eternal life' is emphatic in the Greek, and Jesus may have had a saying of the Rabbis in mind. Rabbi Hillel used to say, 'He who has gotten to himself words of Torah, has gotten to himself the life of the world to come'.

One inevitable consequence of making the traditions of men more important than the words of God is a greater concern about man's opinion than about God's (44). Whenever men judge or approve of one another on the basis of human tradition, it is an indication that they are doing the very thing they would probably deny most strenuously—rejecting the supremacy and sufficiency of the Scriptures. Writing about youth work on Merseyside, Roger Sainsbury says that 'some people have been shocked at the way some of our young Christians still act; they smoke, they drink, they dance to beat music, they don't have regular times of prayer and Bible study. How can they be Christians? Some might even ask. But often their courage in witnessing in most difficult circumstances has put me to shame.'

Learning to distinguish between Scripture and tradition is difficult but essential. Even to insist on as good, as valuable, a 'tradition' as daily Bible reading, as though it were a divinely ordained practice indispensable to Christian faith, is to stand on the slippery slope which led the Pharisees to reject Christ.

For meditation: 'Traditions which are not in conflict with Scripture are permissible if optional. Traditions which are in conflict with Scripture must be firmly rejected' (J. R. W. Stott).

46 : 'Disobedient and Contrary'

Romans 10.1–21

A chapter which is about the Jews' rejection of their Messiah, and is packed full of O.T. quotations, makes an appropriate conclusion to a group of studies on the Jews, the Scriptures, and tradition.

Paul had himself been 'extremely zealous . . . for the traditions of my fathers' (Gal. **1**.14). He knew at first-hand the zeal and the blindness of the Jews. And since he had himself been made righteous by Christ, he has a heartfelt sympathy for those still floundering in the quicksands of human traditions (1, cf. **9**.1–3). Rom. **10** is an expansion of **9**.30–33. Paul's aim is to show his Christian readers that the way of righteousness is open to everyone (5–13); that the Jews have had opportunity to hear the gospel (14–18); and that they reject it because they are 'disobedient and contrary' (19–21). He does this by stringing together O.T. verses, and interpreting them in a manner similar to that of Jewish commentators, but with this vital difference—that he knew Jesus Christ to be the Messiah.

Verse 5, a quotation from Lev. **18**.5, appears to support the Jews' conviction that the law could give life, in contradiction of John **5**.39. The verse should be understood both in the light of Luke **10**.28, where the first commandment—Love God—is the way to life, and also in the light of Paul's own experience of failure to love God and obey His law. It is significant that he chooses another passage from the law of Moses (Deut. **30**.11–14) to illustrate the opposite of v. 5, and to show that righteousness is available to all through faith in Christ. There are important parallels between v. 12 and **3**.22 ff. and between v. 13 and Joel **2**.32 with Acts **2**.21.

In the second part of the chapter, the texts Paul uses answer four points. Everyone must hear the gospel (14 f.), but not all for whom it was intended have accepted it (16 f.). Then have those who rejected it not heard it properly (18), or not understood (19 f.)? It all leads up to a grim warning, particularly for those who believe, as the Jews did, in the full authority and inspiration of Scripture. They were neither ignorant nor stupid, but disobedient and stubborn. In spite of all God gave them, they still missed the heart of the matter.

Questions and themes for study and discussion on Studies 41–46

1. Why, how, and when should false teachers be corrected?

2. What is the value and importance of tradition in the Christian life?
3. Was it true of the Jews, or is it true of Christians, that 'to be the inheritors of a great tradition gives men heroism, and it gives them blindness of heart' (Gore)?
4. How do you reconcile the apparent contradiction between Rom. **3**.31 and Rom. **10**.4?

CHARACTER STUDIES

47 : Lot's Last Chapter

Genesis 19.1–30

Lot chose the way which led to Sodom. He pitched his tent toward the city, and like a magnet the city drew him. He became a citizen, and 'sat in the gate' as a magistrate. His family were immersed in the wickedness of the dark, luxurious little town as their sombre ending shows.

And disaster fell on the valley floor. A fanciful Russian has suggested that space visitors exploded surplus atomic fuel there, and left a record of supernatural visitants to Sodom and grim retribution. The city's fate needs no such interpretation. Warning certainly came to Sodom, and Lot was urged to flee. He did, reluctantly, as the volcanic fountains broke their bonds, and Sodom rocked under the combined assault of earthquake and volcano. Lot's wife looked back, lingering no doubt in anguish, as the scene of the life she had come to cherish flamed amid the spouting gas. Caught in some red hot mass flung from the buried seabed of some earlier salt sea, she became a 'pillar of salt' and a perennial warning for those who fail to make good a prompt escape when catastrophe threatens a corrupt, disintegrating world.

In the hills, safe on his upland pastures, Abraham looked south, and the smoke of Sodom rose 'like the smoke of a furnace'. Some mighty spectacle of ascending conflagration held him spellbound. Perhaps some great mushroom cloud arose from the valley, as oil, freed deep in the earth's scar, flared in the volcanic fires. Certain it is that the whole area is burned and scorched to this distant day, and that the great rift in the globe's skin must bring the surface down near the beds of fuel which are rich throughout the Middle East. No great shock would break open the old wound and set the world bleeding its inflammable oil.

So perished the 'cities of the plain', and with them the land's fertility, its tropic wealth and garden green. And like Lot's wife, the towns became a proverb, and one of them a name for perversion, a 'hissing', as the later prophets of the Hebrews say.

Peter says a good word about Lot (2 Pet. **2**.7), but 'just' though the backslider may have been, he had no influence among those with whom he had chosen to link his destiny, and in his lamentable weakness lost his wife, his daughters, and his place in history. Much evil can flow from weakness, from one carnal choice, from one failure to grasp God's opportunity. It was a vital day when Lot and Abraham stood together on the ridge.

48 : Abraham's Lapse

Genesis 20

A map will add significant details to this story. Abraham at the time was dwelling in the Negev, and his nomadic life was dependent upon water, upon rainfall in a word, and the periodic variations of climate. The coastal plain, agricultural, and commonly the first recipient of the Mediterranean rain-belts, was a natural refuge when the hill-country suffered from a spell of drought.

Gerar lay at the foot of the hills, and was in the hands of the Philistines, those European colonists from Crete, who had a colony on the coast long centuries before the disasters which befell their homeland swelled the settlement to the size of a nation. The ruler of Gerar, some tribal prince, bears a Hebrew name both in Abraham's and Isaac's time (Gen. **26**), and Abimelech is probably a Hebrew translation of a royal title, so that the ruler who encountered both father and son in similar circumstances is not necessarily the same person.

Abraham, long years before, had learned the lesson of such subterfuge as he now practises again, but it is the way of men to repeat their mistakes—'the burned fool's bandaged finger,' as Kipling put it, 'goes wobbling back to the fire.' The patriarch, in a moment of panic, under some stress of testing, again earned the rebuke of an alien. Curiously enough, he retained for his family the respect of the community he had wronged, and this fact is testimony to the completeness and honesty of the repentance which healed the fault. The next chapter shows Abimelech manifesting deep confidence in Abraham and trust in his plighted word (**21**.22–34). A lapse of faith can only be remedied, as Abraham had remedied it after his lamentable retreat to Egypt, by a wholehearted return to the position abandoned in fear, doubt, or transient disillusionment. 'It is the greatest and dearest blessing God ever gave to man,' said the good Jeremy Taylor, 'that they may repent; and therefore to deny or to delay repentance is to refuse health when brought by the skill of the physician—to refuse liberty offered to us by our gracious Lord.' And this applies to the old, equally with the young. No age is exempt from temptation, fortified against all failure, or immune from man's old infidelity—backsliding. Such is the lesson taught in the language of his pain by 'the Father of the Faithful'.

49 : Abraham's Sacrifice

Genesis 22.1–19

In a case in the British Museum stands a small statue of a goat caught by its large horns in a flowering tree. There is a small oblong base, decorated with silver plate and mosaic in pink and white, and on it, erect on its hind legs, stands the goat. The front legs are bound by silver chains to the delicate golden branches of a tree which rises in front of him, a stylized object with a short firm trunk and two geometrical boughs.

The leaves and flowers, all in gold, rise higher than the goat's golden head. There is hair of lapis lazuli, the blue silicate which figured widely in Sumerian art. The sculptor has contrived to represent the hair or wool of the body in shell. This little work of curiously fussy art throws some light on the tale of Abraham.

To Abraham, in the grip of his great idea, one common feature bound mankind together, the baseness of a universal polytheism, and the horror of the world's sanguinary cults.

Obeying a Voice within which had become a part of his faith, he had left the busy town and set out to found, as we have seen, in the clean desert, a race dedicated to the service of the One God.

No man pursues a project of faith without his days of doubt, and there came a time when Abraham became obsessed with an awful thought. The Voice which had so surely governed his conscience took on strange tones. Unbelievably, it bade him to sacrifice his son, even as he had seen children die in the pagan city from which he had retreated in loathing. Abraham, convinced that this terrible pressure on the mind must have a meaning, set out to obey. He set up the altar, he placed the wood, he bound his son . . .

Then, unmistakably, all was clear. There was 'a ram caught in a thicket' hard by. The Voice was strong in command. God, even as Abraham had told his son, had provided the sacrifice. Part of Sumerian belief must have been that an animal so imprisoned had been claimed of heaven as a sacrifice. Abraham recognized the Divine provision, performed the ritual, and found his mind for ever freed from the fear that God might indeed demand a parent's ultimate sacrifice. His obedience had been complete. The race he founded was commanded to write that salutary liberty into the law which became their way of life (Exod. **20**.13). To those who read the Old Testament in the light of the New, another meaning emerges—the substitutionary death of Christ. Abraham knew nothing of this.

50 : Abraham the Businessman

Genesis 23

The Bible does not pretend to present a consecutive history of the men and women who made its story. It did not set out to provide the raw materials of history for historians unborn. It selected its incidents, and families such as Abraham's preserved the record of events necessary for their future guidance. The chapter is by way of being a record of the title to the cemetery of the clan at Hebron, bought from the tough Hittites.

Abraham was obviously a wealthy man. Hebron, Beersheba

and Gerar were key points on the caravan routes, and although there is no mention of such business and trade transactions, it is obvious that the patriarchal community were engaged in the legitimate commerce of the trade-routes of Palestine. From what other source could have come the considerable amount of silver with which Abraham lightly paid for one small lot of ground? James Kelso points out that 400 silver shekels 'the current market rate' (16), was an exorbitant price, when, 'for similar Palestinian real estate' Jeremiah paid only 17 silver shekels. Perhaps it is not legitimate to compare land values separated by such a lapse of time, especially when the latter took place during a period of war and enemy occupation, when land prices would have fallen heavily, but it does seem clear that the shrewd Hittite, after the elaborate Eastern interchange of courtesies, took from the rich desert-chief an inordinately large sum of money.

Observe Abraham's courtesy. A person's character is sometimes best observed from its reflection in the lives or attitudes of others. The previous chapter reveals the polished deference of the prince of Gerar towards the man who, on their first encounter, had disappointed and harmed him. The present scene is similarly instructive. Abraham knew that he was being overcharged. That was one reason why he had the document of sale drawn up with elaborate detail (17), and with proper witnesses (18). He judged haggling beneath his dignity, and, in its ancient context, discourteous. He was a stranger in the land. He had God's word that the land should belong to his descendants. Until such consummation he recognized the rights of its occupants, observed their laws, and conformed to their courtesies. A testimony is worth some outlay in cash and it was a testimony that Abraham sought to establish in the alien's land. There is no outward sign of true courtesy, said Goethe rightly, 'which does not rest on a deep moral foundation'. The grace of God is in courtesy.

51 : Abraham's Servant

Genesis 24

We have spoken of the mirror-image of a person's life which can be seen in the character of another. The servant of this charming chapter, besides being a gracious person in his own right, reflects very vividly the fine master he serves. 'We become willing servants to the good by the bonds their virtues lay upon us,' said Sir Philip Sidney, and in Eliezer of Damascus Abraham had a willing servant of the sort which only goodness could produce.

Abraham had done more than inspire the loyalty and faithfulness which enabled him to entrust a delicate and vital mission, together with a considerable sum of money, to a steward's care. He had transmitted his faith to his man. And yet a faith which was no mechanical lip-service to a God imposed upon him. No one can doubt, in the words of the servant's prayer, the reality and personal understanding of the faith he cherished. He sought guidance with a plain simplicity of language, observed with wonder the working of God's hand in circumstance, and gave thanks for the miracle. Abraham, the man of faith, had proved the reality of his faith by passing it so potently to one who served him.

Observe his loyalty. The servant, we have reasonably assumed, was the Eliezer of **15**.2, named heir of Abraham, according to well-attested custom. Such adoption was null and void on the birth subsequently of an heir, and Eliezer had been supplanted, it would appear, by Isaac. His loyalty was in no wise diminished. If the assumption is mistaken, and the envoy to Bethuel was not Abraham's one-time heir, his loyalty is still a shining virtue. Loyalty, ran a Roman saying, is the holiest good in the human heart. It is the test of love, for loyalty is steadfastness in performing love's obligations. Loyalty is the chief mark of unselfishness, for it must disregard personal advantages in furthering the interests of its object. It is a jewel in a treacherous world. So Milton pictures the seraph Abdiel:

. . . Abdiel, faithful found
Among the faithless, faithful only he;
Unshaken, unseduced, unterrified,
His loyalty he kept, his love, his zeal.

Love, zeal, piety mark the servant who took the caravan train to Haran. He is a good man to know. With his act of efficient, sensitive and selfless service he disappears from history, but not from the approval of God—'Well done, good and faithful servant.'

52 : Rebekah

Genesis 24.15–67

Rebekah, or Rebecca as the New Testament, following the Vulgate, spells her name in its only reference (Rom. 9.10), was the daughter of Bethuel, Abraham's nephew. She moves gracefully into the charming story of this chapter, like some maiden, exquisitely carved, from the frieze of the Parthenon. Yet such a simile falls short, for Rebekah is no marble figure, but warm and vital. We meet her busy about the tasks of the household, spontaneously courteous and hospitable, and ready to go a second mile in generosity (19 f.). Active and vigorous, she added eager energy to her natural attractiveness, no withdrawn, proud, and self-conscious beauty, but ready to display, at some cost in time and in strength, the hospitality of desert peoples to the wanderer and the stranger in the land. It is a good daughter who reflects the virtues of her house (25).

There are days in life which are a hinge of our fortunes, and it is well to treat each day as if it contained eternal consequence. This was Rebekah's day. Abraham's dignified and devoted servant was taken home to the house of Bethuel, and stated his errand. Bravely Rebekah recognized the movement of God's hand, and faced calmly the unknown future. She had, as a girl should, prepared her heart and mind for the fulfilment of marriage. It is a natural ambition, a worthy goal for which the normal man or woman plans. It involves a major choice in life, a choice faced and made with small experience, and under the urge and thrust of the deepest of the heart's emotions. Cold reason takes second place, and it is well for those who move into life's longest partnership to do so with the consciousness of God's guidance, and with passion disciplined by virtue, unselfishness, and a desire for God's will. Rebekah seemed taught in such matters, made her choice with calm decisiveness and simplicity (58), and departed on her high adventure.

And yet there is sadness in the story, for the idyll ended. Disappointment was to try Rebekah sorely, and perhaps a certain rift of understanding came between the young wife and a husband twice her age. Was love complete when loyalty died, and husband and wife were sundered in their lamentable favouritism? Life has no more sombre sight than promise faded, than first love grown cold, and later years which disappoint and fall short of all that might have been. Testing and trial, borne together and in mutual trust, need not spoil and weaken.

53 : Isaac

Genesis 24.62–67; 25.19–26; Psalm 105.1–11

Isaac is a somewhat elusive and colourless character among the patriarchs. It is almost as if he had lived so long under the shadow of Abraham that he had failed somehow to develop a sharp and decisive individuality. His virtues are passive ones. We meet him at the close of the romantic story of Rebekah walking in quiet meditation on the desert sand as the stars come out. We met him earlier in the grim story of Abraham's temptation on Moriah, where the marks of his character, seen behind the words of the narrative, are vivid—utter obedience to his father, complete faith (Abraham had passed this quality well and truly to his son), and full surrender to God's will. Isaac emerged from that ordeal 'born again'. He had lost his life to find it again.

Isaac was forty years of age when he married. There is no reason at all why a marriage between a man of that age and a girl like Rebekah should not be happy and successful, but it calls for adjustment and understanding of a sort to which, perhaps, judging by the sequel, Isaac and his bride did not rise. We are told that Isaac loved Rebekah (**24**.67), and in the briefly traversed story of their early years of union (**25**.20 f.) Isaac's concern for his wife's great disappointment is evident. But was the gulf, in their case, bridged?

A stronger man might have bridged it, but Isaac, faithful, devout and submissive, had not, perhaps, those more active qualities which could have compassed this end. Abraham may have been to blame for some fault here. We have seen his anxiety for the line of his descent, upon which his whole vision for God's new race depended. He may have delayed too long his son's marriage in this live concern, a delay meekly and characteristically endured by Isaac. Parental dominance can be too overpowering. To protect one's sons is good and godly. To stunt their growth, like that of a plant that grows in the shade of a tree, is disservice.

Matthew Arnold touched the thought in *Rugby Chapel,* when he wrote of his great father's death:

For fifteen years,
We who till then in thy shade,
Rested as under the boughs
Of a mighty oak, have endured
Sunshine and rain as we might,
Bare, unshaded, alone,
Lacking the shelter of thee.

Did Isaac wilt in the sun and rain when the great oak of Mamre fell?

54 : Abraham's Son

Genesis 26

This is a very sad chapter. Isaac's folly in falsely describing Rebekah as his sister is psychologically true to form. This is no mistaken repetition of an old tradition. It illustrates too exactly, and too sadly, Isaac's subservience to his father, and the unhealthy dominance of a great man over his weaker son. Abraham had done precisely this, and, in a moment of apprehension and of stress, his son followed the same pattern of deceit, and earned the same embarrassing reproof from a pagan.

Isaac was weak, and it is not long before the arrogant recognize weakness and take advantage of it. Colonists from Crete, as we have already seen, had a foothold on the southern coast of Palestine. They were called Philistines, a cultured European people, and had actually given Palestine its name. There is a perennial hostility between Lowlander and Highlander, and the shepherds of the hills were often at odds with the townsmen of the plain. It is evident from the story of the disputed wells that the plainsmen were on the offensive, and were actively pushing the Hebrews back into their hill-country and wilderness hinterlands. Such was history's first confrontation of Asian and European.

Isaac, typically, retreated, and at last, in the deep desert, found rest. Rehoboth means 'broad places', or 'room'. The Israelis have a dry-farming research-centre on the site. Here Isaac felt he could breathe unmolested. And God demonstrated His care for the man of peace. So to move out of an atmosphere of hostility and strife was manifestly His will. He renewed His covenant with Isaac, and so blessed him that the alien sought his friendship and alliance.

But catch the note of pain at the chapter's end. Esau, demonstrating his lack of sympathy with his family's ideals, married a Hittite, and gave her the Hebrew name of Judith. To give a name does not change a character, and the intruder 'made life bitter' for her parents-in-law. There are few sins more contemptible. To be a good son or daughter to the parents of a wife or husband is no betrayal of one's own people, but a source of satisfaction, a cementing of friendship and a rich reward. This situation should have been demonstration enough to the head of the clan that Esau was not likely to be a suitable successor. But we shall see the sequel.

Questions and themes for study and discussion on Studies 47–54

1. What was Lot's basic fault?
2. Is there anything to learn from Abraham about prayer?
3. What did the Lord mean by: 'Consider Lot's wife'?
4. Are lies ever justified?
5. What has the New Testament to say of Abraham in three epistles?
6. List Abraham's testings.
7. How does religion enter business?
8. What are the chief qualities of 'a good and faithful servant'?
9. What place has loyalty in marriage?
10. To what extent is protectiveness a parental virtue?

THE GOD WHO SPEAKS

Christ's use of Scripture

55 : In Temptation

Matthew 4.1–17

In 'The Heart of the Hunter', the explorer Laurens van der Post describes the hard experience of being alone in the vast empty spaces of Central Africa, and its effect on people. 'To be in the wilderness,' he says, 'especially alone, is a fiery test of a man's inner life.' When Christ went through that fiery test, fiercely assailed by Satanic temptations, it was the word of God in the O.T. Scriptures which sustained Him and provided His answers to the temptations.

Christ knew the O.T. so thoroughly that there is great variety in His use of quotations. Sometimes they must be understood in the light of the original context and sometimes not, but it is worthwhile and important to study the context every time. Normally the temptations are understood with reference to Christ's mission as alternative ways of working—a Christian Aid miracle man, a popular wonder worker, or a political compromiser. This interpretation is one of the many probable meanings of the temptations, but it takes little account of the chapters in Deuteronomy from which Christ's answers were drawn. A careful examination of Christ's replies to the temptations, seen in their contexts, may open a deeper level of interpretation. The first answer (4) is from v. 3 in Deut. 8.1–10 which is based on Exod. 16 and 17 The Israelites in the wilderness certainly needed bread but when they were in a tight corner, with supplies running out, would they rely on the word and the command of God, and trust Him, or start a revolt? Christ, facing the same temptation, trusted God's word.

The second answer (7), from Deut **6**.16, also reflects Exod. **17**. The people were not content with what God chose to do. They wanted proof that He was with them, so they had the nerve to put Him to the test (cf. Mark **8**.11–13). Jesus did not require such proof. What God chose to do was sufficient for Him.

The third answer is from Deut. **6**.13 in the context of vs. 10–15. The people of Israel were to enter a good land, but they would be surrounded by pagans. Would they serve God alone, or compromise? Again Jesus faces a similar temptation. For Him, God alone was more than sufficient.

Seen in the context of the experience of the people of Israel, one part of the meaning of the temptations is relevant to almost every Christian individually and to every Christian community. Few are tempted to perform social or economic miracles, or become the talk of the town by hurling themselves off London's Post Office Tower, trusting in God's care. A great many are tempted to doubt or question the Word of God, the actions of God, and the sufficiency of God.

For meditation : 'I have laid up thy word in my heart, that I might not sin against thee' (*Psa.* **119**.11).

56 : In Teaching

John 10.22–39

Whether He is in acute spiritual danger in the wilderness, or in danger of death by stoning in Jerusalem, it is through the Word of God that Jesus masters the situation. The Jews, despite their devotion to the Scriptures, were getting desperate. Was Jesus the Messiah or not (24)? The answer Jesus gave, which led up to a claim to be equal with God, provided them with an ideal opportunity to solve everything with some well-aimed stones (30 f.).

The quotation of Scripture which Jesus used to persuade them to drop the stones was just five words long and seems obscure to us. To the Jews it was a notoriously difficult verse.

In Psa. **82**.6 it referred to the judges who were charged with administering justice in accordance with God's Word. They were people 'to whom the word of God came' (35) and as such, were called gods (cf. Psa. **82**.1). That being so, Jesus could hardly be guilty of blaspheming for calling Himself 'Son of God' (36).

To the Jews the verse was a problem because it was not easily reconciled with the uncompromising monotheism of the law. Hence Jesus' reminder to them—'scripture cannot be broken' (35). In John's Gospel, 'Scripture' indicates a particular passage; and the word 'broken' means ignored or set aside. The force of the saying is that even so brief and difficult a verse cannot be set aside since it is part of Scripture. It is of great significance that Jesus should make even so brief and controversial an O.T. saying the nub of His argument. The fact that He does so indicates that He shared the Jewish view of the full authority and inspiration of the whole of the O.T.

For further study : 'St. John records the permanent significance of the O.T. no less than the Synoptists' (Westcott). With John **10**.35, cf. **13**.18; **17**.12; **19**.24, 28, 36.

57 : In Controversy

Matthew 22.23–46

Both the Pharisees and the Sadducees distorted or blunted the truth of God's Word, the former by submerging it in tradition and the latter by superficial interpretation. The question in vs. 24–28 is typically fanciful and legalistic. It is based on a baldly materialistic way of interpreting Scripture, and while it purports to reflect faith in God's Word, it is an expression of unbelief; they do not know the power of God. Christ does not accept their statement, not even as a half-truth. He rejects it as untrue, and refutes their false deduction from Deuteronomy by a proper deduction from Exod. 3.6. His interpretation is based, not on the surface meaning of the passage, but on the principle behind it.

While the Sadducees are temporarily silenced, the Pharisees seize their chance. Their tradition included hundreds of commandments, and the Palestine Department of Employment must have suffered an appalling loss of productive man-hours while the Pharisees debated the relative importance of them. Verse 36 reflects this debate. Christ's answer, another quotation of Scripture, takes them back to basic principles. Its effect is like a flame-gun going over a patch of dead weeds.

With both the Pharisees and the Sadducees silenced, assuming the latter were still around, Jesus leads them to think again about the Messiah. Once again He uses the Scriptures, a psalm well-known and widely-discussed by the Rabbis. Their 'idol' was a warrior-Messiah, a King like David, whose son he would be. 'But David called him Lord,' Christ points out; 'If David used the divine name to describe the Messiah, how can the Messiah be David's son?' It is such a clear, honest and straightforward understanding of Scripture that it is hardly surprising they stopped questioning. Perhaps they started thinking.

To think over: 'It is by a constant self-criticism of our own idolatries that we Christians can learn again and present to our contemporaries the glory of God in the face of Jesus Christ' (A. M. Ramsey).

58 : Basic Principles

Matthew 5.17–26

Like the foreword to a book, vs. 17–20 set out some basic principles. They explain in advance points which might otherwise be seriously misunderstood. The rest of Matt. 5 must be read in the light of vs. 17–20. It would be easy, and it has often been done, to interpret vs. 21–48 as a new law, contrary to the law of Moses, and aware of this possibility, Christ warns people against thinking that His teaching contradicts the O.T. (17). Verses 18 f. would have been echoed by the Jews of Jesus' time; Josephus, the Jewish historian, writing in the 1st century, says 'We have given practical proof of our reverence for our own Scriptures; for although such long ages have now passed, no one has ventured either to add or to remove or to alter a syllable; and it is an instinct with every Jew, from the day of his birth, to regard them as the decrees of God, to abide by them, and if need be, cheerfully to die for them. Time and again ere now, the sight has been witnessed of prisoners enduring tortures and death in every form in the theatres, rather than utter a single word against the laws and the allied documents.'

It is generally Christian scholars who have over-emphasized what is new in vs. 21–47, taken the teaching of the Rabbis at its worst, and expounded the Sermon on the Mount as a new law. By contrast, the Jewish commentator, Montefiore, concludes that 'Jesus, as the prophetic teacher of inwardness, wanted to show that the true fulfilment of the law included and implied an inward and enlarged interpretation of the leading moral enactments'. When Jesus used the phrase 'You have heard that it was said', followed by an O.T. quotation, it would probably have brought to the minds of His hearers not only the particular law, but also the teaching of the Rabbis on it. He then took the same law, the law He had described in vs. 17–20, and gave an interpretation which, by contrast with current Rabbinic teaching, was 'something finer and deeper, something more inclusive, completing, and profound' (Montefiore).

In Matt. **5** Jesus uncompromisingly endorsed the supreme authority of the O.T., while at the same time penetrating the heart of its meaning.

Questions and themes for study and discussion on Studies 55–58

1. Is it ever right to study a verse of the Bible apart from its context?
2. Study the ways in which Matt. **5**.21–48 fulfils rather than contradicts the law.

THE GOD WHO SPEAKS

The Apostles' use of Scripture

59 : The O.T. in a New Light

Acts 13.16–43

It has been suggested that 'One of the main activities of the Early Church was hunting down prophecies, types and analogies in the Old Testament for the illumination of the mystery of Christ' (S. C. Neill). The suggestion may seem a little far-fetched; surely the Early Church had more important things to occupy them? Were not their main activities worship, evangelism and service? Two weighty factors indicate that Stephen Neill is probably right. The first, already studied, is that the Jews regarded the O.T. as the inspired word of God. Every new happening and every fresh thought had therefore to be either expressly foretold in the O.T. or to be consistent with it. The second, also studied, is that Christ Himself regarded the Scripture as God's word, He frequently appealed to the O.T., and He encouraged His disciples to do the same. The result, further proof of Neill's suggestion, is that at least 10% of the N.T. is made up of O.T. references. One writer has counted 269 direct quotations, and there are several hundred allusions.

It was natural that Paul, speaking in the Jewish synagogues (cf. Acts **13**.15), should appeal frequently to the O.T. The first part of his sermon (16–22) traces the history of Israel through to David. The second part (23–31) follows closely the pattern of Christian preaching which can be clearly seen in other sermons in Acts (cf. **2**.14–39; **3**.13–26; **4**.8–12;

5.30–32; **10**.34–43). Part three details scriptural evidence in support of what has been said (32–41). The purpose of these O.T. quotations is aptly stated in vs. 32 f.; Christian preaching is the good news that what God promised to do, He has now done. The first quotation is from a 'Royal Psalm' (Psa. **2**.7, cf. Heb. **1**.5; **5**.5) and it refers to the day when the King of Israel was anointed as the earthly representative of God Himself and adopted as God's son. The two following quotations confirm that the Messiah is greater than David, since He is to receive all the blessings promised to David (Isa. **55**.3). The final quotation is particularly fitting as the application of the sermon. Its effect upon the Jewish hearers would have been—'The prophets foretold this day; you have looked forward to it; don't miss it.' No wonder they begged to hear more!

Question: What equivalent can we expect today in evangelism, or in the life of the church, to the 'noble' attitude of the Beroeans (Acts **17**.11)?

60 : 'Copies of the true'

Hebrews 8.1–13

The letter to the Hebrews is not one of the favourite letters of the Church today, nor is it generally understood, though it has been described as 'a great and original epistle; the writer had a mind of extraordinary beauty, power and penetration' (S. C. Neill). The reason it is difficult for us to understand is simply that, for the most part, we are not Hebrews. The letter was addressed to Jewish Christians for whom the O.T. was the whole Bible, but 'the interpretation was new; everything was now understood Christologically, and the Old Testament was ransacked to discover the categories in which the reality of Jesus the Christ could be expressed, and to work out the parallels between the mighty acts of God on behalf of His people of old and those new and even mightier acts in which the Christian people felt themselves to be involved' (Neill).

The use made of the O.T. ranges from simple illustration (1 Cor. **9**.9 from Deut. **25**.4) to the more elaborate 'types' in Hebrews. In Heb. **8**.1, the writer begins a summary of the argument of earlier chapters. He points out to his Jewish readers, whose religious life before their conversion had centred on the covenant, the temple, the priesthood and the sacrifices, that Christians have the true reality of all these, The originals were 'copies' and 'shadows'. The 'tent' Moses erected was made according to the 'pattern' (Gk. type) he was shown (5). Between the original type and the final reality there is a direct historical correspondence which guides our understanding. Christ is the true High Priest (1), serving in the real (true) sanctuary (2); He has offered the pure sacrifice (cf. NEB margin, '*have had* something to offer', 3; see **7**.27; **9**.14); He mediates the better covenant (6). He has given the final and true reality to the original types. Significantly, the writer gives a long, direct O.T. quotation to confirm this interpretation (8–12, Jer. **31**.31–34). Types and quotations together emphasize the fact that the O.T. and N.T. are essentially one, to be understood together. Our difficulty with Hebrews is that we are not sufficiently familiar with the O.T. book with which it corresponds, the book of Leviticus.

61 : 'Now this is an allegory'

Galatians 4.21–31

It was C. H. Spurgeon who first popularized the story of the famous tailor whose final word of advice to the 'knights of the thimble' gathered round his death-bed was 'Always put a knot in your thread'. In the same lecture, Spurgeon spoke of illustrations as 'burrs sure to cling to our clothes' when out walking; 'brush as we may, some relics of the fields remain upon our garments; so there ought to be some burr in every sermon that will stick to those who hear it'. Paul's allegory of Hagar and Sarah is just such an illustration. He has argued in many ways in Gal. **1–4** for freedom through Christ and the gospel, as against slavery under the law. This allegory is the knot in the thread. Unlike a type, it does not depend on the original meaning or significance of the O.T. story. It is simply an illustration, and the truth of it depends on other teaching. It is the knot which cannot exist without the thread of truth already set out.

If interpreting the O.T. in this way seems strange to us, it must be remembered that Paul was speaking directly to those 'who desire to be under law' (21). They had four ways of interpreting the O.T., the literal, the suggested, the logical, and the allegorical. Paul, a proficient, well-trained Rabbi, was meeting the legalists on their own ground and offering them what they considered to be the most elevated method of interpretation to confirm his point. By contrast with the elaborate, rambling allegories of the Jews, the Greeks and some later Christians, Paul's use of allegory is remarkably restrained. He uses it only for those familiar with the method, to illustrate rather than to provide a basis for truth.

Question: Can you summarize in one sentence the central point of Paul's allegory, in the light of which the detail should be understood? Cf. **3**.1–14; **4**.1–7.

62 : The Moving Rock

1 Corinthians 10.1–13

The three previous studies which have been concerned with the apostles' use of Scripture have been based on passages addressed to Jews. For them, the O.T. was full of meaning, as it was also for the 'god-fearers', many of whom became Christians. But what of the Gentiles? What use did the apostles make of the O.T. when addressing a mixed church of Jews and Gentiles, such as the church in Corinth? There are several hints in the language of 1 Cor. **10**, quite apart from the substantial use Paul makes of O.T. history. He refers to '*our* fathers' (1), 'warnings for *us*' (6), and '*our* instruction, upon whom the end of the ages has come' (11). There is some evidence that Paul was slightly more restrained in using the O.T. with Gentiles, but not much. In Acts **17**.22–31, for example, when speaking at Athens, Paul did not quote the O.T. directly, but he alluded to it. In his letters to Gentiles, his teaching is full of the O.T.

In 1 Cor. **10**, he uses some events in the history of Israel to provide important lessons for Christians. The Israelites had great privileges, he points out, but still they failed to please God (1–5); and he then spells out and applies the reasons for their failure, concluding with a warning (12) and with encouragement (13). There was a recent example of the value for Christians of such O.T. teaching when the Anglican Church

Missionary Society moved its British headquarters in 1966. The General Secretary, Dr. J. V. Taylor, wrote shortly before the move: 'In recent months my mind has often returned to that very strange reference in the first Epistle to the Corinthians to that supernatural rock which accompanied the travels of the People of God. I presume that St. Paul was taking as his parable the legend which the rabbis passed on that the Rephidim rock from which the waters had gushed forth to quench the thirst of Israel followed them about in all their subsequent wanderings. The idea of the marching rock is not, after all, so weird to anyone who has motored across the plains of South India or Eastern Uganda and seen how one isolated crag seems to stay with the traveller hour after hour. This is an apt and evocative image of that which is permanent and reliable in the midst of change, an image of Christ Himself, but also of the unchanging call of Christ and of that identity which obedience to the call gives to us. The rock symbolizes both the changeless "I am", and also the changeless "Thou art" which God addresses to us. I have always felt it to be significant that when Moses in Midian was confronted with the awful adventure to which God was sending him, his first two questions were: "Who am I?" and in so many words, "Who are you?". Without a sense of identity, without an assurance of what we are meant to be, we become paralyzed and totally unable to go forward into the unknown. And this is a very common malaise of these days.'

Note: While it is possible that Paul had the rabbinic legend in mind, he may well have been speaking metaphorically, 'i.e. wherever the Israelites were, the supply never failed' (IVP, NBC). This does not lessen the relevance of Dr. Taylor's words, but serves to high-light an aspect of the apostle's use of Scripture.

63 : 'For our instruction'

Romans 15.1–13

Again in this passage, as in 1 Cor. **10**, Paul tells both Jews and Gentiles alike that the Scriptures were written for *our* instruction (4). In **15**.1 f., he is completing the argument he has been working out in ch. **14**. The climax of his teaching is the example of Christ, who 'did not please himself' (3). It is extremely unlikely that any preacher or teacher today would want to add anything to that climax, but Paul does. Those three words which occur so often in the O.T.—'It is written'—introduce a quotation which has something to add even to teaching based on Christ's example. Psa. **69** is frequently used in the N.T. (cf. John **15**.25; **19**.28–30; Rom. **15**.3) and the other half of the verse quoted in Rom. **15**.3 appears in John **2**.17. Paul uses the psalm to describe Christ as 'being so identified with the cause of God that He endures in His own person the assaults of the enemies of God' (Dodd). Significantly the quotation refers to Christ's faithfulness to God and its use to confirm the exhortation in v. 2, 'let each of us please his neighbour', implies a close link between obedience to God and consideration for others. In vs. 9–12, Paul again strings together several O.T. quotes to reaffirm the point made often in Romans, that Christ is the servant of Jews and Gentiles alike.

The way he uses these passages of the O.T. is an object lesson in the truth of vs. 4 f. The purpose is hope, the means is steadfastness (cf. 2 Cor. **6**.4, 'great endurance'; Heb. **3**.14), and the encouragement of the Scriptures. The value of the O.T. for us has been quaintly but aptly expressed by Bishop Moule: 'Not only is it, in its Author's intention, full of Christ; in the same intention it is full of Christ for us. Confidently we may explore its pages, looking in them first for Christ, then for ourselves, in our need of peace, and strength, and hope.'

Questions and themes for study and discussion on Studies 59–63

1. What similarities are there between Heb. **9**.11–14 and Lev. **16**.1–14?
2. What lessons are to be learnt from 1 Cor. **10** about the way in which 2 Tim. **3**.15 f. should be put into practice?

CHARACTER STUDIES

64 : Esau the Profane

Genesis 25.29–34; Hebrews 12.16, 17

Esau was a 'profane' person (Heb. 12.16, AV). Profane, in fact, is a good translation, if the word is taken in its literal sense. Its basic meaning is 'outside the temple', therefore 'removed from the sacred', 'unconsecrated'. It applies exactly to Esau. He was outside the circle of his family's faith, aspirations, desires. He was outside the will of God. He had chosen, in his self-will, to stand outside the plan.

The story in Gen. 25, to which we have returned, is abundant illustration of his gross, unsanctified personality. The story of the 'mess of pottage' put a metaphor into the languages of the world, but does not mean that the destiny of Israel was decided over a corrupt bargain and the sale of a dish of lentil soup in a nomad camp in the Negev. The real reason why the birthright passed to Jacob was that, with all his lamentable faults, he did not despise it. Esau did, as the last verse of the chapter points out.

Esau was completely unsuitable for the high task of leadership. He was an earthy, carnal character without finer sensibilities or spiritual insight of any sort. The bargain with Jacob was, in his eyes, a joke. He had no idea what 'the birthright' signified, beyond that it was a formal recognition of tribal leadership. He had no intention of keeping a bargain so ridiculously made, as his later plaint to his father, when Jacob, again deceitfully, had confirmed the transaction, amply shows.

Esau was a man of the flesh, and a slave to strong and

violent appetites. To such characters, consequences, responsibilities, decency, the standing and testimony of the family, God's will and morality, matter nothing when the flesh is calling. They never resist its demands, never recognize a higher calling which enjoins self-control, and the taming of the desires of the flesh.

The end of the story comes two chapters later. To such personalities comes sometimes the realization of what has been done in the heat of passion, the confidence of prosperity, the arrogance of youth, the pride of the heart, or the greed of the body. A 'great and bitter cry' (**27**.34) does not then avail. Life can become a 'mess of pottage' by our folly and wilfulness. It does not satisfy, is transient, and destroys the beauty of God's plan. As the Persian Omar said:

The earthly hopes men set their hearts upon
Turn ashes, or they prosper, and anon,
Like snow upon the dusty desert's face
Lighting a little hour or two, are gone.

65 : Isaac's Family

Genesis 27

The family life of the aged Isaac is an unpleasant picture. Here is the unwholesome revelation of a wife disloyal to a weakening husband, of a man and wife perniciously cherishing their favourites, of an old man who had lost his vision, and of a strong wife who appears never really to have had one.

We have discussed the carnal Esau. His brother was scarcely better. He was self-seeking, crafty, and ready, for his own advantage, to exploit a brother's manifest weakness. His one redeeming feature was that he did, in a dim, perverted way, have some realization of what 'the birthright' meant.

Rebekah had little of such understanding when she sought to secure it for her cunning son. A mother's supreme task is to lead her sons and daughters to God. Her darkest sin is to turn them away from God and uprightness. And no mother can expect her children to rise higher than herself. A Jezebel produces an Athaliah. Jacob matched the treachery of

Rebekah, and his regard for his father was no greater than his mother's regard for her husband. She prompts her son to lie and to deceive, and the vast irony of the situation is that they secure corruptly, and at infinite cost in suffering, what they would have won in any case, had they waited for God's time, and the outworking of God's plan. So, many a 'birth-right' of happiness, joy, fulfilment, in more spheres of life than one, is soiled and spoiled by premature and hasty grasping with lustful hands, what God Himself will give, crowned with His blessing.

To 'do evil that good may come' is a vicious doctrine. Evil produces 'after its kind'. Success, in the worldly sense of the word, is not the supreme good of life. Rebekah lost her son. As far as the record goes, there is no evidence that she ever saw Jacob again. Misfortune dogged Jacob's life, and it was only long years later that he found his peace with God. Amiel, the Swiss philosopher of the ninteenth century, rightly said : 'Woman is the salvation or destruction of the family. She carries its destiny in the folds of her robe.' The obligation lay more heavily on Rebekah in Isaac's time of obvious decrepitude.

66 : The Aged Isaac

Genesis 27

We must read this fascinating chapter again, because a broken old man sits in the camel-hair tent, of whom we have said little. Isaac, however, is the key to this situation. We have noted his strain of weakness, and this was an element in the sad fortunes of his family. He is old now, somewhat deaf, and totally blind, and a web of intrigue is spun about him by his clever wife, and subtle son.

For himself, Isaac preferred his vivacious, uncomplicated son Esau, who brought good meat into the camp from his hunting in the wilderness. He did not see, or care, that such genial qualities are often shallow and fickle. He had fallen into selfishness in his lonely old age, solitary because fellow-ship with his wife had faded. Preoccupied with her son Jacob, Rebekah had no doubt neglected him and he had become more and more withdrawn.

He had taken to measuring worthiness by what advantage accrued to himself, and vision had so faded and judgement so tragically weakened, that he could bring himself to propose Esau as his heir. He felt no call of God, but sought the stimulus of wine and meat in order to rise to that high level of poetry and prophecy which was the Eastern context of such a ceremonial.

So tenuous was now the thread of God's purpose which had begun with Abraham's call from Ur. So sad was the last chapter of a life which God had once sealed for His own. We should make it our prayer to end well. To know how to grow old is a task for wisdom, the most difficult chapter in the book of living.

There was something, none the less, of the truth inherited from his father left flickering but alive in him. The tragic story of the great deception runs to its base conclusion and at v. 33 Isaac awakes, with a burning blaze of realization, to the fact that the course of folly which he had chosen in self-will, without confiding in Rebekah, and in pure pursuit of favouritism, was not only wrong, but had been taken from his hands. He finds that God has restrained him and produced an end he had not intended. His strong words : 'Yes, and he shall be blessed', mark his repentance for frightful tampering with God's plan. And a frightful thing it is to tamper with God's purpose for our lives—or for the lives of others.

67 : Jacob's Journey

Genesis 28

With typical deception Rebekah secures the safety of her favourite son. She never saw him again. There is a touch of pathos in v. 9. Left alone now with his parents, Esau seeks to please them, and perhaps clumsily to remedy his earlier error by marrying a girl less alien to their kin (26.34).

Jacob sped north, following the mountain spine of Palestine. For all his treachery and double dealing, he had 'the root of the matter in him', as Bunyan put it of another. He was on his way to the old homeland of his family, and the memory of his grandfather Abraham was alive in his mind.

This is surely demonstrated by his dream. He had heard perhaps tales of the ziggurat of Ur, the great artificial hill of cubed masses of brick, topped by the temple of Ur's chief goddess, and housing some of the priestly corporation which controlled much of Ur's irrigated farmland. Up the side climbed a steep stairway, the remains of which are still to be seen. Perhaps Abraham's last view of his hometown across the level desert, in the clear air, was the ziggurat, with the far specks of distant humanity visible on the stair.

Did this become a child's imagery of heaven and the way up and down thereto? It was still a living image in Nathanael's prayer almost two millennia later, when the Lord uttered a mysterious word to him, only to be understood in the terminology of the prayer under the fig-tree, of which only Christ and Nathanael knew (John 1.51).

Jacob needed help. There was enough of reality in him to cause him to turn to the one-time source of help. He sought the God of Abraham, and from the depths of his mind the dream drew the image of the way to heaven. No one reaches for God without God reaching in strong response to him, and Jacob, for all his unworthiness, was granted a renewal of the ancient covenant.

Like the followers of the Lord Himself he misconstrued the proffered Kingdom in terms of his own advantage. He bargained foolishly with God, but he was determined to return to the land of destiny. Fortunately, God's guidance and God's blessing do not depend on the clarity or the unselfishness of our understanding. The spark was dimly burning. Over long years, and through manifold suffering, God fanned it to a flame.

68 : Jacob in Exile

Genesis 29

This is a strangely touching and human chapter. Jacob's love for Rachel, and the pathos of Leah's unmerited rejection, make a moving story. There is also the dark threat of Laban's deceit.

Observe the old-world hospitality which was part of the character of the peoples of the wilderness, the river plain and the ancient caravan trails. Hospitality is a mark of character, for it is fed by graciousness, activated by unselfishness, and adorned by courtesy. We have seen Abraham dispense it, and Abraham's servant receive it, in the very place where Jacob is now so generously received.

'The polite of every country,' said Goldsmith, 'have but one character. A gentleman of Sweden differs but little, except in trifles, from one of any other country . . .' Jacob comes very near to us in these moments of polished courtesy. Courtesy is the patina of culture. It is the first casualty when culture decays.

But there was another sphere, not so heartening, in which Jacob also received that which he had himself bestowed. He had dealt deceitfully with Esau, and now, at a high and vital moment of his life, he is himself the victim of an act of cruel deception. It was bitter pain for both the girls. It was a blow for Jacob, who must have remembered and recognized the misery he had himself inflicted. Commonly in life double-dealing returns upon itself. The continuing story shows that Jacob was far from purged of his old fault. In Laban, however, he had met another who was his match.

The worst of all frauds is to deceive oneself. All sin comes more easily after that, and Jacob was perilously near the point where he was his own victim. There is one safe course only in life, and constitutional deceivers like Jacob find it difficult to accept the fact. That course was well laid down by Ruskin: 'Do not let us lie at all. Do not think of one falsity as harmless, and another as slight, and another as unintended. Cast them all aside. They may be light and accidental, but they are ugly soot from the smoke of the pit, and it is better that our hearts should be swept clean of them, without one care as to which is largest or blackest.'

69 : Jacob's Prosperity

Genesis 30

Like the nation which was to spring from him, Jacob had to endure a long period of servitude. It is not possible to disguise the fact that Jacob was little more than a bond servant of his father-in-law for a full twenty years. It was in God's plan. Spoiled and protected by his mother, Jacob needed this weathering of character. He needed the taste of his own brew of duplicity. Laban was a harsh burden, but, like many people, Jacob needed the experience of such a man about him.

His family-life was a sad one, and a grim indictment of any other system of marriage than that which owns and reveres Christian values. Poor Leah poured her grief into the names of her first three sons. Reuben (Look! A son), Simeon (he—presumably God—hears) and Levi (meaning doubtful, but possibly 'joined'). Later Levitical law forbade such bigamy of jointly living sisters (Lev. **18**.18). The hate-filled rivalry of Jacob's household provides a reason for the prohibition. The disgraceful rivalry in child-bearing extended to the 'giving' of servant maids, as secondary breeders, doubtless with Jacob's base compliance, and reference to the folly of his own grandfather, who had similarly invoked old Sumerian law. The rill of God's purposes through the race of Abraham was again tenuous. And yet this Jacob was to be Israel.

The device which Jacob employed to gain material advantage at Laban's expense was superstition. There is no genetical basis for the practice, and the increase of Jacob's holdings over those of Laban must have been due to some providence of God to provide the wherewithal for the exodus to Palestine. So often men attribute to their own clever devising that which is in fact the gift of God's grace.

Jacob's swindling was none the less true to form. That Laban richly deserved such disloyalty was no excuse. In fact the wheel had come full circle again. 'Man never fastened one end of a chain around the neck of his brother,' said Lamartine, 'that God did not fasten the other end round the neck of the oppressor.' Laban was now to feel the tug of the chain with which he had bound Jacob. Jacob might have awaited rescue by worthier means, but he had not yet learned to 'leave it all quietly to God' (Psa. **62**.5 in Moffatt's rendering. The whole psalm is a comment on Jacob's adventures).

70 : Jacob's Return

Genesis 31

There is little new in this chapter, but it is a vital link with the next great movement in Jacob's life. He had deceived

Laban, and there was hot anger in the tribe. It was well to have out upon the surface that which was active underneath, and the hostile atmosphere around him decided Jacob that the time was ripe for a return to the Promised Land.

Perhaps there was little noble in his motives. The territory of Laban had become a difficult place, and like the Prodigal Son Jacob sought the father's house. But it was a move in the right direction, and God seems, in His grace, to accept the smallest of motives for action in the right direction. Besides, we have seen that there was, deep down beneath all the clutter of selfishness and sham in Jacob's life, some knowledge of the purpose of God in His people and in the land. He seemed conscious of the pull of God's will, and could hear God's voice—when it suited him to hear.

The memory of Bethel remained with him, and Bethel may be thought of as Jacob's experience of conversion. He could not but see the purpose of God in sending him into exile. After his cynical deception of Isaac he had been pulled up by the roots, and God sometimes does this to shake the dirt from the roots. The process had not been notably complete in Jacob's case. Bethel could have been the beginning of a changed and ennobled life. Conversion, notwithstanding experiences of a 'second blessing', can and should be an embracing experience of transformation. In too many cases, and Jacob's was among them, the divine encounter effected but a partial change.

He brought more useless trash back from the Euphrates than Laban's stolen idols. He still bore the load of his deceitfulness. It had paid him well in the sort of advantage that Jacob understood. He was still fond of material things. He had won them in abundance. Men commonly get out of life what they seek with all their heart. The question is what those things are worth in the end. Read 1 Cor. 3.11-20. Jacob was very soon after Laban's departure to have a striking illustration of this truth.

Questions and themes for study and discussion on Studies 64–70

1. How far and when should evil be actively resisted?
2. What has the New Testament to say about 'alien' marriage?

3. What of favouritism in a family? Are there other Biblical examples?
4. List some other mothers of Scripture, notable for good or ill.
5. What is our 'birthright'?
6. How is it possible 'to tamper with God's purpose'?
7. How much is faith a prerequisite for God's guidance?
8. What place has hospitality in a Christian's testimony?
9. 'To have done with lying is the beginning of all virtue.' Discuss this.

THE GOD WHO SPEAKS

Principles and Problems

71 : Supreme Authority

John 17.1–19

The key words at the beginning and end of this passage, authority (2, Phillips) and truth (17), sound strange among the discordant noises of popular thought. Today's theme words are tolerance and synthesis; 'the open mind has become a yawning chasm,' writes Richard Hoggart, and 'truth' lies in a futile piecing together of the ideas of men.

The word translated authority or power (2) 'is a very comprehensive term and excellently suited to express the idea of an all-inclusive authority, in the sense of the freedom and the power to command and to enforce obedience, and to have possession of and rule and dominion over' (Geldenhuys). It is used in Matt. **21**.23 where the chief priests ask Jesus 'By what authority are you doing these things, and who gave you this authority?' The answer, which they were not given at the time because they were not able to receive it, is that Christ was given authority from God the Father, authority 'over all flesh, to give eternal life' (2).

Yet though He has power to enforce obedience, Christ does not do so. He is not an authoritarian figure, compelling obedience and enforcing submission without regard for individual freedom. Christ's authority is to *give* eternal life, not to force it on people. 'As a redeeming authority, it says "Be free and obey." It does not say, "Obey and be free."' (Forsyth). This is precisely the sort of authority which people need and which many today are feeling after. It is against authoritarian rule, whether in politics, university or Church, that people rebel.

Christ expressed this redeeming authority by giving to the disciples the words of God (8, 14). He claimed that His words were the words of the living God, and that He spoke not with human authority, but with the authority of God Himself (cf. **12**.49). It is all summed up in v. 17, 'thy word is truth'. All the words of God form a single, sufficient, coherent whole, which is not merely true, but truth.

For meditation: Consider the four consequences which flow from the words of Christ—faith (7 f.); *joy* (13); *opposition* (14); *dedication* (18 f.).

72 : 'Even so I send you'

Galatians 1.1–2.2

The roots of the authority of the apostles are indicated in John **17**.8. They had been given the words of Christ, they had received them, and they believed and knew the truth. They knew that Christ was Himself *the* Apostle (Heb. **3**.1), sent from God. When the Risen Christ showed Himself to them and commissioned them (John **20**.19–23), they in turn became Christ's apostles. Their authority was accepted in the Early Church, and to the question—'What happened to their authority when the apostles died?'—the answer is that apostolic authority remains where it always was, in the apostolic word. The Scriptures contain both the apostolic witness to Christ and their instructions for the life of the Church, which the early Christians received as the words of Christ Himself (1 Thess. **2**.13; 2 Pet. **3**.2).

The dispute in some churches was over the authority of Paul (cf. 1 Cor. **9**.1 f; 2 Cor. **12**.11–13; 1 Tim. **2**.7). The basis of the uncompromising apostolic authority which he exercised was his experience on the Damascus Road, and it is that experience which underlies this passage in Galatians. Paul almost certainly knew the facts of the gospel before he set out for Damascus (13). He had listened to Stephen and probably to other Christians. What he needed to know was the truth and the meaning of those facts, and that is what Christ gave him in a blinding moment of revelation (12). When he saw and heard the risen Christ, Paul knew that reports of the resurrection were true. God had raised Him. The curse of death on a tree had been transformed into a blessing (3.13 f.).

This revelation did not itself make Paul into an apostle. A comparable, if less dramatic, vision of Christ has not infrequently been a feature of the conversion of Muslims. Paul not only saw Christ, thus becoming a witness to the resurrection, but he was also specifically commissioned by Christ to be an apostle to the Gentiles (16). Paul's apostleship is therefore set on precisely the same basis as that of the other apostles.

In 1.18–2.2, Paul emphasizes that his knowledge is independent of, but consistent with, that of the other apostles. He knew the truth direct from Christ. He was an apostle by the direct action of Christ (1). But he was also humble enough, and wise enough, to make sure that his gospel was the same as that preached by the other apostles. Like them, Paul could and did claim that he spoke with divine authority (2 Cor. 13.10; 1 John. 1.5).

For meditation : 1 *Thess.* 2.13.

73 : 'As originally given'

1 John 5.1–12

It is one thing to recognize that the original words of the Scriptures have divine authority. Whether the text of the Bible as we have it is precisely the same as the original words of Scripture is another question altogether. The phrase which appears in some doctrinal statements concerning the authority of the Bible, 'as originally given', is a straightforward recognition of the fact that some error has crept in as the text has been passed on. How, and how much?

The two passages chosen to illustrate this problem are both worth studying as a whole for what they say about God's Word, but the particular textual point of interest in 1 John 5 is in vs. 7 f. The AV is significantly different from later versions. It includes the words 'there are three that bear record in heaven, the Father, the Word and the Holy Ghost: and these three are one'. And after the words in v. 8, 'There are three witnesses', it adds 'in earth'. John Stott describes the whole of this addition as a gloss, and he points out that 'the words do not occur in any Greek manuscript, versions or quotation before the fifteenth century' (Tyndale Commentary, p. 180).

What may have happened is that a studious monk added what he thought was a helpful note in the margin of his copy of 1 John, and the scribe who copied the manuscript later included the note in the text. Great care was taken in copying manuscripts, but mistakes were sometimes made—such as the inversion of letters, 'scared' for 'sacred'; the omission of a word, such as 'not' in the commandment concerning adultery in the 'wicked' Bible; the addition of words, such as 'and fasting' in Mark **9**.29; or the substitution of what is familiar for what is unfamiliar.

The RSV and most other recent translations do not even include the extra words of 1 John **5**.7 f. in the margin, as these translations are based on more complete and more accurate manuscript evidence. The verses, though still difficult, are easier to understand without the monk's tidy gloss, which Stott describes as 'not a very happy one'. 'The threefold testimony of verse 8 is to Christ; and the Biblical teaching about testimony is not that Father, Son and Holy Spirit bear witness together to the Son, but that the Father bears witness to the Son through the Spirit.'

For study : Does the comment on v. 8 *apply also to the witness to the truth of God's Word?* (*cf. John* **16**.12–15).

74 : A Thousandth Part

Revelation 1

The hymn 'With harps and with viols', which is always sung with such gusto by Welsh choirs, has a chorus based on Rev. **1**.5—'Unto Him who hath loved us and washed us from sin . . .' The word 'washed' appears in the AV; in the RSV, it is 'freed'. The difference of a word in English is only a letter in Greek, *lusanti*—freed, or *lousanti*—washed. It makes a significant though not a vitally important difference to the meaning.

The word 'freed' is more generally accepted as being the original, not because it appears in more manuscripts, but because it appears in those that are most reliable. Students of the text have to try to trace the pedigree and assess the value of the different manuscripts; they cannot solve all problems simply by counting the number of times different readings appear and accepting the one which appears most often, since any number of manuscripts may copy one wrong one. In his biography of Asquith, Roy Jenkins describes the break-up of relations between Asquith and Lloyd George in 1916. His main source is Beaverbrook's 'Politicians and the War'. There are other books on the subject, but as Jenkins points out: 'almost all lean heavily, with or without attribution, upon Lord Beaverbrook's version. . . . It is therefore often the case that, at first sight, a statement appears to be overwhelmingly confirmed from about six different sources; but on closer examination, the six sources all turn out to be subsidiaries of the central Beaverbrook fount.'

The impression could easily be gained that the whole text of Scripture is in the melting pot. Nothing could be further from the truth. The famous Cambridge Greek scholar, Hort, estimated that differences in the text made up no more than a thousandth part. No major doctrine is disputed because of doubt about the text. By comparison with documents of similar age, it is remarkably well-preserved.

This is no more than we should expect. There would be little point in the Spirit telling John to 'Write what you see in a book and send it to the seven churches' (11) if the Spirit did not intend ensuring that it would reach not only the seven churches but ourselves as well, for whom it was also intended.

For further study: As with 1 *John* **5**, *the passage chosen to illustrate one textual point has a great deal else to say about God's Word; see especially vs.* 1–3 (*cf.* **22**.16–19).

(Other aspects of Rev. **1** will be the subject of a later study.)

75 : History, Legend or Myth

Genesis 3.1–21

Any great complex of literature brings together many different literary forms—historical narrative, poetry, legend, myth, letters, parables—and it is of great importance that each form should be interpreted on its own terms. Parables should not be treated as historical fact; legend should be understood as an interpretation of and witness to the truth of history; while a myth may be treated as having no connexion with history at all. 'The word myth is used of those majestic tales, such as the early stories in Genesis, in which a profoundly religious understanding of the human situation, such as can hardly be better conveyed than through such a tale, is made known to us' (S. Neill). On that understanding, Genesis **1**–**3** may be understood without any reference to history at all.

This approach is only possible if the way in which the N.T. interprets Genesis is ignored. From Gen. **1** and **2**, the N.T. teaches that the human race is 'from one' (Acts **17**.26); and the offence is of one man (Rom. **5**.12–19) who is 'as distinct an individual as were Moses and Christ. These guidelines exclude the idea of myth and assure us that we are reading of actual, pivotal events' (D. Kidner, Tyndale O.T. Commentaries). Similarly, with regard to Gen. **3**, the N.T. assumes and argues from the historical reality of the Fall (cf. Luke **3**.23 ff.; Rom. **5**.18 f.; 1 Cor. **15**.20 f.).

If Gen. **3** is not myth, what sort of history is it? Kidner suggests a possible answer in a parallel between Gen. **3** and two chapters in 2 Samuel. In 2 Sam. **11**, which is historical fact, an account is given of David's sin against Uriah. 2 Sam. **12**.1–6 puts that same history into legend form in order to interpret it. The question is—is Gen. **3** equivalent to 2 Sam. **11** or 2 Sam. **12**.1–6?

76 : Contrasts

Matthew 28.1–8; Luke 24.1–11

The narratives of the resurrection pose in an acute form the problem of disagreements in Scripture. The accounts attest vividly the central fact, but there are several differences of detail. A careful comparison of all four accounts reveals that different groups of women come; they come at different times; details about the stone and descriptions of the messengers are not the same; and in Luke **24** and John **20**, Jesus appears in Jerusalem, while in Mark **16** and John **21** He appears in Galilee.

There are two ways of approaching this sort of problem. The first is to attempt to harmonize the facts and make all four accounts into a single coherent record. Geoffrey King's

'The Forty Days' is a good example. This approach is valid up to a point, as major discrepancies, sufficient to cast doubt on the credibility of the record, could not be tolerated. Even so, attempts to harmonize every detail of the resurrection accounts are generally remarkable more for their ingenuity than for the conviction they carry. The historical reliability of the Bible does not depend on the successful harmonization of every detail of differing accounts.

The second approach is to understand the documents and explain the origin and significance of the differences. The Gospels do not record the findings of a Royal Commission appointed to inquire into an extraordinary event. They tell us how the fact was first realized. In the Early Church, the fact of the resurrection would be told, together with a detailed description of what happened, to one or two witnesses. Gradually, the main centres of Christian life—Jerusalem, Caesarea, Rome, Ephesus—would accumulate their own accounts, preference being given to the narratives connected in any way with local people. The four evangelists, when they came to write, recorded faithfully the accounts given at the centres with which they were associated. Each writer gives an incomplete account; probably all four accounts together do not include all the details.

Such differences as these confirm rather than deny the central fact. Exact correspondence in every detail arouses suspicion rather than belief. In a famous tribunal of inquiry concerned with methods of police interrogation, one member of the tribunal said, in giving judgement against the police, 'The mechanical precision with which the chief police witnesses corroborated every detail of each other's statements cast suspicion upon their evidence.' No such suspicion attaches to the accounts of the resurrection.

77 : Self-Consistent

Matthew 25.31–46

Again and again in Christian history, and especially in recent theological writing, these verses have been interpreted in a way which suggests that they contain the whole of Christian faith. A Jewish writer, C. G. Montefiore, says of vs. 33–40, 'The charity rendered, the loving service paid . . . is regarded by

Christ as if rendered to Himself. There need not even be the conscious thought that it is done for Christ or in His name. This is splendid doctrine. The loving deed is enough. No purer account, no more exquisite delineation of Christian philanthropy was ever penned. It is broad, liberal and truly religious.' On the face of it, these verses set OXFAM supporters, 'Shelter' helpers, and prison visitors, Christians and non-Christians, on the same basis—that of judgement by works and not by faith.

The two principles of interpretation which must be remembered in studying a passage like this are the self-consistency of Scripture as a whole and the importance and value of each section. God's word is truth—one part of Scripture does not contradict another; and 'every inspired scripture is profitable', including the genealogies.

The total understanding of Scripture, within which the interpretation of Matt. **25** must be set, is that the N.T. teaches two truths with equal emphasis. First, we are made acceptable to God only by Christ—'it is God who puts us right' (Rom. **8**.33)—and not by anything we do. Secondly, it is by what we do that we are recognized as God's. Both these truths are clearly taught by Christ and by the apostles. Both are evident in the Gospels and in the writings of Paul and James. A passage like Matt. **25** or Jas. **2**, which concentrates on the second truth, must be set alongside the first, without being either ignored, diluted, or misinterpreted.

It is possible that in all the discussion about reconciling Matt. **25** with Christian theology as a whole, the heart of the passage is missed. It 'should be understood as Jesus' farewell speech to His disciples. The accent falls not so much on the surprise (37–39), or the unconscious goodness or badness; that is only a rhetorical device which gives further weight to the sentences repeated in vs. 40 and 45. Thereby Jesus, at His departure, makes the rank-and-file brother in need His representative; He identifies Himself with him' (K. Stendahl).

Questions and themes for study and discussion on Studies 71–77

1. What is the relation between the teaching of Jesus as recorded in the Gospels and God's authority today?
2. How and to what extent was Jesus influenced by the times in which He lived, and what effect does this have on the authority of His teaching?

CHARACTER STUDIES

78 : Jacob and Esau

Genesis 32.1–21

It is worthwhile to look at a map. Laban had pursued the fugitive caravan southward, and come upon it in the highlands east of Jordan called Gilead. It was rough country and there was rougher still beyond. South of Gilead lay one of the eastern tributaries of the Jordan, the Jabbok stream, which flowed in a deep dark gorge under the shadow of the Gilead uplands down to the river. It was probably the gorge up which David struggled in the last lap of his retreat from Absalom centuries later. David was to make his headquarters at Mahanaim (Twin Camps), which Jacob named next day. It was here, after Barzillai's feast, that David probably wrote Psa. **23**, and it was no doubt the dark Jabbok ravine which gave him the imagery of the 'valley of the shadow of death'.

It was such a valley to Jacob. From the northern slopes, with Laban gone, Jacob looked south to a new life and the land of his birth. His projected path was probably along the route of the present highway from the Dead Sea to Amman, for Jacob seems to have purposed crossing the Jordan where the Allenby Bridge crosses it today, near Jericho. But between Jacob and the life he hoped to renew was a looming obstacle. He had seen it rising on the skyline for some days—the blue mass of the Mountains of Moab, which flanked the road, the river and the salt Dead Sea. And this was Esau's territory.

Jacob was mortally afraid

The ghosts of forgotten actions,
Came floating before his sight,

And things that he thought were dead things,
Were alive with a terrible might . . .

It is one of the penalties of evil that its consequences lie in ambush down the path of life.

Note Jacob's action. His whole subtle mind was active in his self-defence. He approached Esau with polite diplomacy (3 f.), but was dismayed to hear that his wronged brother was on his way to meet him with a considerable force. He arranged his company for rapid dispersal and flight. Then, with all his organization complete, having the assurance of God's presence (1 f.), he turned to prayer (9–12). In spite of his own unworthiness (10), he knew that God honours obedience (9) and fulfils His promises (12).

79 : Jacob's Wrestling

Genesis 32.22–33.17

Jacob had his 'mess of pottage' back. He knew how fragile was all material prosperity. In one hour it could all belong to Esau, with his own life forfeited, or spared for penury and slavery. He was alone in his suffering, for he had achieved no fellowship with his wives. In the hour of his mind's agony he could only send them away (**32**.23).

Left alone by the Jabbok, Jacob met the Guardian of the Land, identified in Hos. **12**.3 f. The whole terrible struggle was God's battle with Jacob to bring him to surrender. He had just been shown in stark horror how weak, how little, he was, and how worthless all those goods he had striven for with subtlety and selfishness over many years. But there was to be no entry into the promised land for the old, soiled Jacob. God was presenting His ultimatum. Jacob had made his typically clever and deceitful arrangements to impress his brother with his might and wealth, but God did not intend to allow Jacob to begin a new chapter of his life on the slim foundations of trickery.

There comes a time in the life of those who inadequately follow God when He demands reality. He tolerates half-heartedness and carnal discipleship to a certain point, and then suddenly He confronts the selfish follower with the challenge which tests sincerity. God had long enough been pressing hard upon Jacob's uncommitted life. Conscience, riding beside him, had been calling ever louder to him, 'Surrender!' Now, with crisis in the morning, the time had come for the last struggle. Jacob, like many another, had wondrous power in resisting God.

The way to win in any wrestling with God is to surrender. God won. Jacob, calm now, and prepared still to trust and follow, whatever Esau did, is given a new name (2 Cor. **5**.17). When wrestling with God changes to clinging to God, God will act.

Day dawned. Esau came. None of Jacob's fears materialized. It was a facet of Esau's earthy personality that he bore no grudge. Jacob, like some Christians, was shamed before the greater worth of one who made no high pretensions. The caravan moved on. Silent, humble, subdued, Jacob rode in its midst. He crossed the river a cleaner man.

80 : Jacob's Harvest

Genesis 34

It is part of the frankness of the Bible that it speaks of the sins and the follies of those that make its story, as well as of their qualities of good. This chapter is an ugly tale, and one which the reader might gladly pass by, but it is part of Scripture and must be faced. This was the material with which God was compelled to work. Is it much better today?

In the old Scofield Reference Bible this chapter was headed: 'Jacob reaps the harvest of his evil years' (Gal. **6**.7 f.). It is sombrely appropriate. Here is our first contact with Jacob's sons. Over the next fifteen chapters we come to know them as strong, ruthless men, whose path to God was as rough, twisting, and difficult as their father's had been.

Jacob was in many ways to blame. No man can expect his sons to be better than he is himself. By the mercy of God they sometimes are, but it is not in human power to lift another beyond the level of one's own attainment in spiritual matters. For long, vital and impressionable years these men had watched their father's life. They had seen his reliance on subtle dealing, and their own brutal and sanguinary treatment of their neighbours was nothing more than a version of their father's trickery. A family sometimes has its own way of applying to circumstances the principles it has picked up in rudimentary form from its parents' conduct and example.

Complete obedience on Jacob's part might have preserved the men from the temptation, for it was his choice which determined the circumstances of the atrocity which they committed. Jacob was Israel now, and a full understanding of the Covenant might have dictated a return to the clean Judean hills where the separate life of the tribe and its Abrahamic faith could have been developed free and apart from the contaminating influence of pagan neighbours, and the presence of the Canaanitish towns.

Old nature died hard, and lifelong habit had taught Jacob to seek advantage. The fertile vale of Shechem was better grazing, and more comfortable country than the harsh uplands of Judea which Abraham had chosen when Lot moved down to Sodom, or the southern desert round Beersheba where Isaac sought refuge. Shechem and its perils need never have entered the lives of Jacob's sons had it not been for Jacob's choice of a dwelling place.

Hence tragedy, and a stain upon Jacob's name among the inhabitants of the land. Remember Abraham's care for their presence. The phrase of his grandfather, uttered to Lot, stuck in Jacob's mind. The situation was a grim reminder (13.7).

81 : Back to Bethel

Genesis 35

The crime of Jacob's sons had roused the hostility of the land, and it was only the restraining hand of God which quelled the movement which rose against the intruding tribe (5), now on its way back to the place of blessing. Bethel was a symbol in Jacob's life. His return to it was a renewal and a recommittal. It is sometimes necessary in human experience for the soul to seek the old sources of its strength and vision. Abraham did.

Jacob began with some determination. We begin to see in him the marks of the new life which began when he surrendered completely to God on the banks of the Jabbok in the night encounter. God re-emphasizes to him that his name is new (10). This is no repetition of a story. It is psychologically apt, and no sign of the clumsy editing of some old corpus of Hebrew tales. Jacob was given his new name by the Gilead stream. All deep experience needs feeding. Jacob was a better man but no man attains perfection in sudden flight. We too commonly 'wrestle on towards heaven 'gainst storm and wind and tide', and Jacob, even in his new role as Israel, had already made one major error. He was, like many of those who read about him, to make more. The task, for those who fall, is to rise again.

It was a good beginning, none the less, to cleanse his camp of the remaining vestiges of idolatry. His women, notably Rachel, had retained remnants of old paganism. All spiritual advance begins properly with such cleansing. The 'strange gods' of such a purging are unearthed in numbers by Palestinian archaeologists. They are the common fertility symbols of sex-ridden and perverted cults.

They have their modern counterparts. If a parent purposes to lead his family 'back to Bethel', the place of renewal, rededication and old vigour, it is sometimes necessary to get rid of the family idols. 'Little children, keep yourselves from idols' (1 John 5.21), are probably the last words to be written in the Bible. And 'idols' are not always obscene figurines of baked and painted clay. They can be possessions of more than one form, pursuits and preoccupations, ideas, and pleasures—anything, in a word, which usurps the supreme place in a life. They block the path to Bethel and at all costs must be cast aside.

82 : Esau Again

Genesis 36

This chapter might easily be passed by in a study of the characters of Scripture were it not for a tragedy embedded in two verses. Esau has been dismissed as a profane, an irreligious and carnal man, and in his early years the record has shown him insensitive to his privilege, and to the great purposes of God working out in Abraham's children.

And yet there is also evidence that Easu contained good human material, had someone known how truly to love him. Isaac's love was selfish. Rebekah, in her blind favouritism, did not love him at all. Jacob saw him as a rival. (The phrase, 'I have hated Esau' [Mal. **1**.2 f., cf. Rom. **9**.13], was not, of course, a denial of God's own nature. In Semitic thought the phrase only means: 'To Esau have I given second place in my purposes'—and that was Esau's choice.)

There are several hints at Esau's hidden worth. His cry of pain, when he found that Isaac had given the blessing to another, is an indication of a sensitive heart behind the bluff and unrevealing exterior. When he met Jacob south of the Jabbok, he was a generous brother, with no revengeful spirit harbouring the rankling memory of old wrongs. He makes a pleasant impression.

The first of the two significant verses mentioned is v. 6 in this chapter. Esau retreated from his brother's presence. He could have remained in the land, even if, with the gentler outworking of God's purposes, he had at last been brought to see that Jacob should be the spiritual leader of the tribe. Esau would have doubtlessly been given a noble role to play. Jacob had made it impossible for him to remain in the place of blessing.

Verse 6 again shows the sensitivity of Esau's character under the rugged façade. Here was a life damaged by another, a 'drop-out', if that word may be used, from the plans and purposes of God. But no one can so withdraw without becoming a menace. Verse 43 is the second verse which, we have suggested, is significant in this chapter. Read, in some Bible dictionary, what harm the people of Edom did to Israel. List prominent Edomites. It is a sad pity that, through the clumsy selfishness of an unconsecrated mother and brother, a man of worth and ability was harmed and spoiled, and driven from the place he might have occupied, and the usefulness he might have known.

Questions and themes for study and discussion on Studies 78–82

1. What five things are most worth seeking in life?
2. What is 'carnal' Christianity?

3. How do prayer and organization mingle?
4. Consider the last view of Esau. What of unlikeable Christians?
5. What is the secret of parental influence? What of heredity and environment?
6. What are 'strange gods', 'idols', in modern experience?
7. Name some prominent Edomites.

THE GOD WHO SPEAKS

Understanding Scripture

83 : Understanding O.T. History

Exodus 15.22–27

Countless sermons on the cross have been preached from this straightforward historical narrative, with v. 25 as the focal point. 'Some', says Matthew Henry, 'make this tree typical of the cross of Christ, which sweetens the bitter waters of affliction.' Another commentator makes no mention of the historical situation in Exodus, or of the meaning of the event for Israel, but concentrates exclusively on a figurative interpretation: 'The tree is the picture of the cross . . . the cross was cast, as it were, by God into the bitter waters of the world . . . it was the means of making the bitter waters sweet and turning death into life for all who believe.' Is this interpretation legitimate?

Two guidelines for interpreting O.T. history can be illustrated from this passage. The first is that the narrative must be studied in its original setting; what were the circumstances and what did the event mean for those involved at the time? The people were desperate for lack of water—three days of sand and sun were more than enough (22); and when they found water, it was unfit to drink. The people murmured, Moses prayed, and God 'showed him a tree', one which may have had special natural properties with which some Arabs today are familiar. The primary and central lesson is that God is to be trusted, 'acknowledged not only in the creating of things useful for man, but in discovering their usefulness'

(Matthew Henry). Many other direct lessons could also be drawn from the passage, all from historical understanding of the original meaning.

The second guideline is that figurative or allegorical interpretations of historical narrative are possible if they are consistent with scriptural truth as a whole. Christ's use of the brazen serpent and Paul's allegory of Hagar and Sarah are examples (John **3**.14–15; Gal. **4**.21–31). The difficulty with this sort of interpretation is that it can lead to all sorts of wild and fanciful ideas, and a useful rule is suggested by A. M. Stibbs: 'Such practice needs to be employed only with great restraint and wherever possible, with confirming scriptural justification. Otherwise it gives unlimited scope to arbitrary fancy, and opens the door for men to read into Scripture almost anything they wish to see there.'

Question: Is there sufficient 'scriptural justification' for interpreting the tree as the Cross?

84 : Understanding N.T. History

Mark 4.35–41

The principles which apply to the interpretation of O.T. history apply equally to the N.T. Like Exod. **15**, Mark **4** has been given both strictly historical and marvellously fanciful interpretations. The three questions to ask about a particular passage of N.T. history are what is its significance in the particular setting (is there some word of explanation from Jesus, or a reaction from the crowd)? What is its meaning in the total ministry of Jesus, or in the life of the Early Church? And what is its bearing on life today?

In Mark **4**, there is both an explanation and a reaction (40 f.). 'What is the matter?' Jesus asks. 'Don't you know who I am? Don't you trust me?' 'Who is this?' the disciples wonder, awestruck. 'Even wind and sea obey him.' The primary meaning is clear; Jesus is Lord of Creation. He is able to control nature. To the disciples, such power could mean only one thing—Jesus must be God. But at that early stage in His ministry, such a conclusion was too much for them; the event was one among the many evidences which led them eventually to acknowledge Jesus as God's Messiah. The passage has the same primary and central meaning for us today; it is one part of the evidence for believing in the deity of Jesus. The original historical meaning is still significant today.

There have been plenty of figurative and allegorical interpretations of the passage. The most common is that of Tertullian: 'that little ship represented a figure of the Church, in that she is disquieted in the sea, that is, in the world, by the waves, that is by persecutions and temptations, the Lord patiently sleeping, as it were, until roused at last by the prayers of the saints, He checks the world and restores tranquillity to His own.'

Question : more difficult than on Exod. **15** *! Is there scriptural justification for Tertullian's interpretation ?*

85 : Understanding O.T. Prophecy

Amos 9.11–15

Men of equal conviction about the inspiration and authority of the Bible, of equal ability in their understanding of language and meaning, and of equal devotion to Christ, have come to different conclusions about the interpretation of prophetic scriptures. That fact underlines the need for careful study, humility, and restraint.

It is important to recognize that prophets spoke about past, present and future events. It is necessary therefore, as with historical narrative, to understand the prophecy in its original setting and to study its meaning for the people to whom the prophet spoke. The last words of Amos' prophecy would have given the Jews a glimmer of hope to gaze at while the grim events of the rest of his prophecy took place. Verses 11–15 would have been appreciated by them as 'a very pleasant piece of music, as if the birds had come out after the thunderstorm and the wet hills were glistening in the sunshine' (Adam Smith).

After studying the verses in their original historical context, the possibility of later fulfilment in Christ or of direct application to our own times should be examined. The prophets spoke for their time and for the future, but often without any awareness of possible fulfilment centuries later (cf. 1 Pet. **1**.10–12). Amos **9**.11 was quoted by James at a critical moment in the life of the Early Church as the pivot of his judgement about the admission of Gentiles to the Church (Acts **15**.16–18). There is no doubt about the scriptural justification for this interpretation!

86 : Parables

Luke 16.1–13

No less than one third of Jesus' recorded teaching consists of parables—about 60 of them in all. C. H. Dodd gives an instructive definition : 'A metaphor or simile, drawn from nature or common life, arresting the hearer by its vividness or strangeness and leaving the mind in sufficient doubt about its precise application to tease it into active thought.' That last part fits precisely the experience of the disciples; 'Now you are speaking plainly, not in any figure!' they said in relief on one occasion (John **16**.29). They would have totally rejected any attempt to explain the parables as simple moral tales.

Some principles of understanding parables stand out from the story of the dishonest steward. The first is that parables are not allegories. Some, like the sower, or the wheat and the tares, may allow for the interpretation of every detail, but most teach one main lesson. If the dishonest steward is treated as an allegory, the result is hopeless doctrinal confusion.

The second principle is that we must study parables in their historical context. Some knowledge of first-century business methods is essential to a full understanding of the dishonest steward (which emphasizes, incidentally, that we do not honour Christ by simply telling without explanation the parable of the lost sheep to Merseyside children who know nothing about sheep or shepherds).

The key to the interpretation of the dishonest steward is v.8. The steward pulled a fast one on his master. He was dishonest; what he did was sharp practice. He is commended for 'prudence' (8), for shrewdness. He is not himself a pattern for Christians, nor is his dishonesty, but his shrewd use of money is. Verse 9 sums up the lesson for us: 'Show that you are Christians by using money. Don't bury it—use it to serve people. And when money no longer counts for anything, the people you have served with it will be waiting to welcome you into eternal life.'

As is often the case with a parable, the verses which follow (10–13) do not interpret or explain it; they expand and develop it. To interpret a parable in the light of succeeding verses can be misleading.

87 : Paul's Letters

2 Peter 3.8–18

It should not surprise us that the quick, volatile mind of Paul, and his mercurial personality are so clearly apparent in his letters. We have already noted that God uses rather than 'takes over' personality.

Peter was by no means the last Christian to utter a perhaps slightly regretful warning on Paul's letters (15 f.). Dr. H. Chadwick mentions a number of theologians who 'were not always certain that they understood him and even, at times, wished that the apostle had sometimes expressed himself with more caution and finesse'. He quotes a most significant and instructive comment from one Methodius in the third century: 'You should not be upset by the sudden shifts in Paul's arguments, which give the impression that he is confusing the issue or dragging in irrelevant material or merely wool-gathering. . . . In all his transitions he never introduces anything that would be irrelevant to his teaching; but gathering up all his ideas into a wonderfully harmonious pattern, he makes all bear on the single point which he has in view.'

The 'ignorant and unstable' twisted Paul's letters by taking one part and ignoring others. They concentrated on 'free grace' and wallowed in total permissiveness, forgetting the clear moral implications of the gospel (cf. Rom. 6); or they missed the central issue and lapsed into bondage (cf. Gal. 1.6). But while every Christian may find Paul's letters hard to understand, it is only the 'ignorant and unstable' who 'twist' them to 'their own destruction'. Ignorance and instability are to be countered by a continual growth in knowledge and grace (18).

88 : Visions and Symbols

Revelation 1

One of the greatest living preachers, Helmut Thielicke, says of Revelation, 'The last book of the Bible remained obscure and dark for centuries, and now all of a sudden, amidst the catastrophes of our time, it is as if the dark wraps had been removed from this book and the broad landscape of history is plain and in it the wonderful highways of God, all of which by roundabout ways lead to the distant, blue hills from which cometh our help.' That may be so, but Revelation remains one of the hardest books in the Bible to understand.

It is usually described as apocalyptic, the Greek word for revelation, meaning literally to unveil something previously hidden. Vivid word-pictures and symbols are used to represent truths, some of which could not be openly stated for political reasons (cf. parts of Daniel and Ezekiel, e.g. Dan. **7**). The meaning may be for either the present, or the future, or both. Rev. **1**.1 indicates that the book had an immediate relevance to first-century Christians; the word 'soon' must be given its due weight (cf. vs. 3, 19 and **22**.10). This means that, as with history and prophecy, the first step in understanding is to examine the actual situation to which the book spoke.

On this basis, remembering the harsh persecution of the Church by the imperial power towards the end of the 1st century, we look for truth which would strengthen God's people then—and in subsequent ages. The opening chapter sets the pattern and theme for the book; vivid imagery and symbolic language are used to capture a most striking and evocative vision of the risen, victorious Christ. No mention is made of the Satanic powers, the enemies of Christ's Church, who feature prominently in later chapters. Since the book is to show that Christ is the Victor, the Conqueror, who has the keys even of death and Hades (18), and that He remains victorious even when His Church seems to be defeated, it is highly appropriate that the opening chapter should be dominated by this vision of majesty and glory. Again and again throughout the book, glimpses of this vision are given (**2**.8; **5**.9 ff.; **12**.9 ff.; **14**.1; **20**.4; **22**.3). Christ 'conquers death, Hades, the dragon, the beast, the false prophet, and the men who worship the beast. *He* is victorious; as a result, so are *we*, even when we seem to be hopelessly defeated' (Hendriksen). Difficult problems of interpretation in later chapters ought not in any way to obscure the central figure, the Risen Christ, whose word is 'Fear not, I am the first and the last'.

Questions and themes for study and discussion on Studies 83–88

1. What specifically Christian teaching may be illustrated from the account of Noah's Ark, and what is the O.T. justification for it?
2. What are the main similarities and differences between prophecy and apocalyptic, and how should each be understood?
3. What light do Mark **4**.10–12 and Matt. **13**.34 f. throw on our understanding of parables?

THE GOD WHO SPEAKS

Obeying God's Word

89 : From Faith to Faith

1 Corinthians 2.1–16

In theory at least, it would be possible, though difficult, for a person who had neither driven nor even lifted the bonnet of a car to understand a technical book about the workings of the internal combustion engine. A person who attempts to understand a religious document without himself holding the religion set forth in it faces far greater difficulties. In theory, perhaps, it ought to be possible: in practice, adherents of a faith see it in a different perspective from that of outsiders. Christians have made some remarkably sensitive attempts to understand Islam, though a Muslim would find fault with even the best expositions. But when Paul talks about 'spiritual truths to those who possess the Spirit' (13) he is not talking of the differences between those who do something and others who merely study it, nor of the difference between 'insiders' and 'outsiders'. He is talking of entirely different kinds of people, those who are 'natural' (14) and those who are 'spiritual'. The verses clearly refer to regeneration. It is only those who have been 'born anew' by the direct action of God's Spirit who can understand spiritual truth (cf. John 14.26; Rom. 8.14–17). The reason for this is indicated in vs. 6–12. The Christian message is not a word of human wisdom. It has not been discovered through human enlightenment, like Buddhism, nor by 'logical' deduction, like humanism. It is the wisdom of God, disclosed to man by God Himself 'through the Spirit' (10).

All this does not mean that the human part of communicating Christian truth can be minimized. The balance between the human and the divine is indicated in vs. 1–5, verses which have too often been interpreted as justification for a presentation of the gospel which is intellectually weak or unrelated to the life of the hearers. What Paul disclaims is 'superiority' in 'words of wisdom'; he resists 'enticing' or 'persuasive' words (4). But he 'proclaims the testimony' (1), concentrating on Christ (2), and he presents a message (4). In Acts **18**, his work at Corinth is described as 'arguing', 'persuading' (4), and 'testifying' (5). For eighteen months, he was 'teaching the word of God' (11). This was the human side of his ministry, which must have been exacting intellectually and physically, but all this was none the less human weakness. It was the 'demonstration of the Spirit' which was decisive. The word indicates 'rigorous proof'. The Spirit was convincing the hearers that the message was not merely historically accurate and intellectually satisfying, but divine truth—truth which was, and is, 'the saving power of God' (Rom. **1**.16, NEB).

90 : Faith in God's Word

2 Kings 4.8–37

One of the simplest, most straightforward explanations of what faith means is contained in the account of Paul's shipwreck. To a group of terrified pagan sailors, who had long since given up hope, Paul says with amazing confidence, 'I have faith in God that it will be exactly as I have been told.' God had told him what would happen and he believed God. His confidence was not in the angelic messenger, nor in the words themselves, as though they had magic power. His trust was in God Himself, that He would do *exactly* what He had said.

The Shunammite woman is a vivid example of the same faith. She had not asked for a son, but obviously she longed for children; the news that she 'would embrace a son' was literally too good to believe (16). The birth of her son twelve months later was only a partial fulfilment of God's word, since the promise of a son meant an assurance that the line of her family would be continued. When the boy died of sunstroke a few years later (18–20), she did not 'accept' his death and go into mourning, as though God had changed His mind. Nor did she do nothing. She acted in faith. She told her husband, who only knew that the boy was off-colour, that 'it will be well' (23). She told Gehazi that 'All is well' (26, NEB). And then she put all the responsibility exactly where it belonged—on the man who had first given her God's promise, refusing to let him go until he had done something himself. Whether she expected Elisha to bring the boy back to life is not clear from the story, but it is clear that she expected something. Death was not the last word. The final word was with God. God never goes back on His promises. What He says He will do, He does.

For meditation: 'Never dig up in unbelief what you have sown in faith.'

91 : 'Today, when you hear . . .'

Hebrews 3.1–19

These studies began, in Heb. **1**, with a question which many people ask; 'Why is God silent?' The answer of Heb. **1**.1–4, that God has spoken and still speaks clearly and powerfully to our age through Jesus Christ, is emphasized again in **3**.1. Jesus is the Apostle and High Priest of *our* confession. The phrase in Heb. **1**.2, 'in these last days', which refers to the time between Christ's birth and His second coming, is crystallized into one word in Heb. **3**, the significant word 'today' (7, 13, 15). The writer, knowing that Christ is the full and final word of God to man, and that in Christ God has said all that there is to say, puts a large, urgent question against every day—'Will today be a day when you hear God's word, believe it, and obey it?' Verses 18 and 19 make the connection between obedience and belief, or disobedience and unbelief, quite explicit. The two words are virtually interchangeable in the two verses.

The nub of the chapter is in vs. 12–15. The warnings are against 'an unbelieving heart' and 'the deceitfulness of sin', without any indication of which might come first. Presumably it may be either. On the positive side, we are to 'exhort one another' and to hold firm to that direct faith we first had. The word 'exhort' is the same as that which describes the Comforter in John **16.** It can be used to describe the encouragements which two members of the same team might call to one another. The phrase 'we share in Christ' needs emphasis in a chapter which is rather sombre in tone. To share in Christ opens up endless possibilities. 'Christians . . . . . can always be expectant because they are living in God's "Today", and there is no knowing what may happen and there are no limits to His grace' (D. Webster). It is important to remember that the chapter is addressed to Christians. It is Christians who are urged to listen to God's voice, to believe, and to obey, and to do it now, today, every day, so long as 'today' lasts (13).

For meditation : 'I have been always looking to the future for opportunities to glorify Thee. I live in the future and not in this day that Thou hast given. A life of dedication I want to have, but I am longing to have it only in the future. I want to make my relations pure, only in the future. I am a Christian in a dream, living in an unreal future world, neglecting the marvellous opportunities Thou offerest me today. Lord, give me the strength to rise above the weakness of 'postponement' and continuously create in me a feeling of 'Life is Today', for tomorrow I may never be' (from Meditations of an Indian Christian).

'TODAY, when you hear His voice. . . .'